Feminine Beauty
in Indian Art and Literature

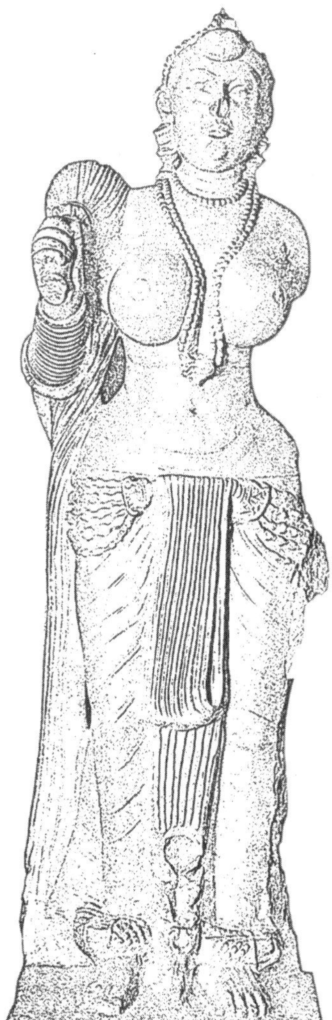

Contours of Indian Art and Architecture, no. 3

Feminine Beauty
in Indian Art and Literature

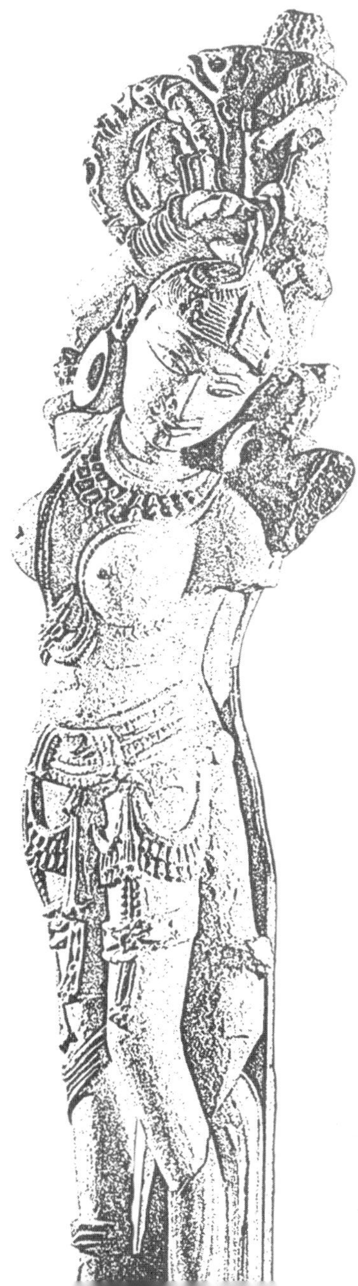

T.N. Mishra

D.K. Printworld (P) Ltd.
New Delhi

Cataloging in Publication Data — DK
[Courtesy: D.K. Agencies (P) Ltd. <docinfo@dkagencies.com>]

Mishra, T.N. (Tej Narain), 1945-
Feminine beauty in Indian art and literature / by T.N. Mishra.
(Contours of Indian Art and Architecture, no. 3)
xiv, 82 p. 25 cm.
Includes bibliographical references (p.)
Includes index.
ISBN 8124603871

1. Feminine beauty (Aesthetics). 2. Feminine beauty (Aesthetics) in literature. 3. Art, Indic. 4. Sanskrit literature — History and criticism. I. Title. II. Series: Contours of Indian Art and Architecture, no. 3.

DDC 701.170 820 954 22

ISBN 81-246-0387-1 (10 digit)
ISBN 978-81-246-0387-1 (13 digit)
First published in India in 2007

Published and printed by:
D.K. Printworld (P) Ltd.
Regd. Office: 'Srikunj', F-52, Bali Nagar
Ramesh Nagar Metro Station
New Delhi – 110 015
Phones: (011) 2545 3975; 2546 6019; *Fax*: (011) 2546 5926
E-mail: dkprintworld@vsnl.net
Website: www.dkprintworld.com

Dedicated to

Amorous Art and Aesthetic Beauty

in

Indian Sculptures

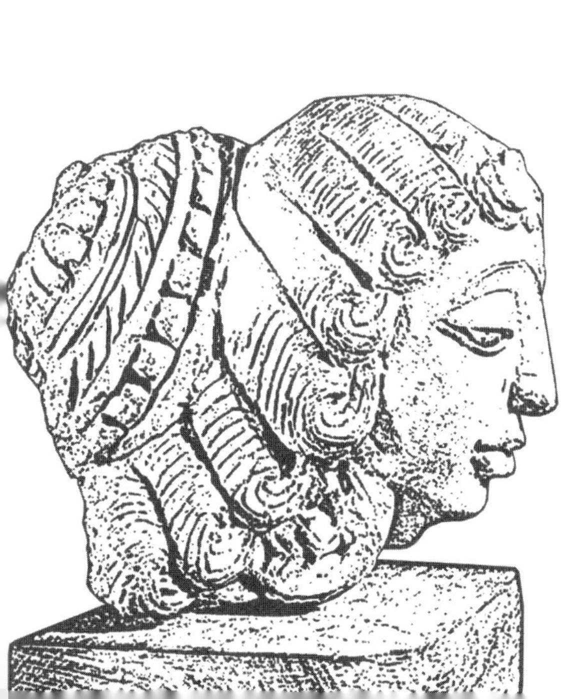

Preface

The history and culture of a nation is known by its art and literature as it mirrors the glory of its past. In India, a very highly and well developed civilization had been flourishing since centuries. It is generally argued that the tradition of Indian art is more ancient than that of other countries. There are evidences of art found at the excavations of the pre-Indus and Indus sites. These excavations provide enough ground to believe that the people who lived there, were not only expert in the building activities but skilful artisans also, with ample evidences of their artistic skill. The Vedic period that followed the said period gave rise to a different kind of culture. The people of this period lived in close proximity with nature and sought its blessings. Men in the past either feared certain forces in nature or propitiated certain elements in nature for their benevolent activities. The fear on the one hand and appreciation of certain forces in nature on the other led to the birth of what we call religion today.

Indian art is from its very inception so intimately associated with Indian religion and philosophy that it is difficult to appreciate it fully, unless one has some knowledge of ideals that governed the Indian mind. The ultimate goal of Indian art had been a kind of

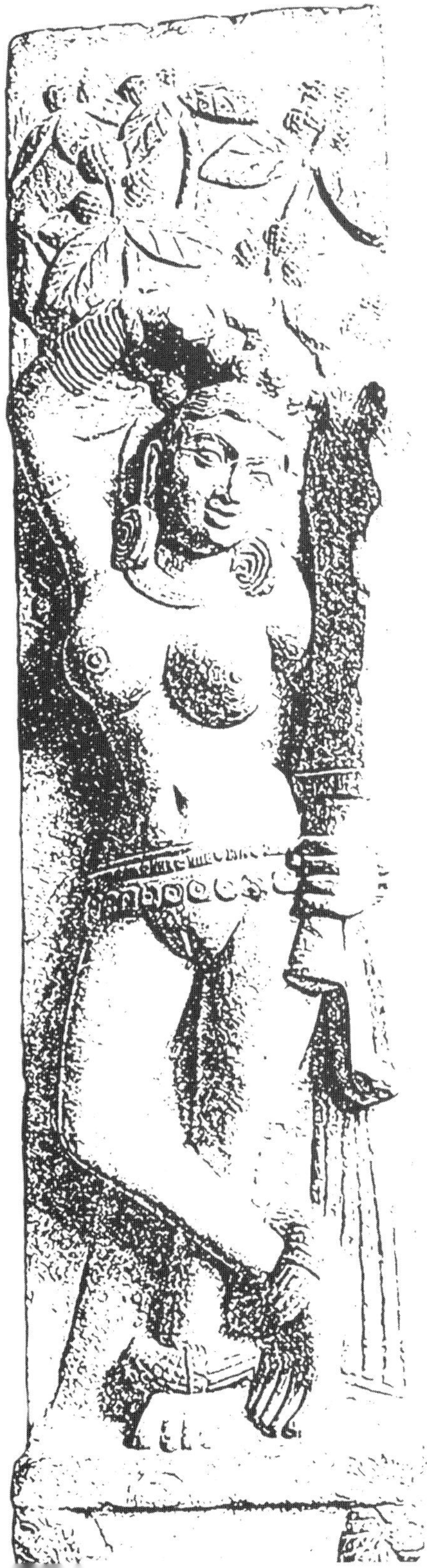

aesthetic enjoyment where there is happy synthesis between the sublime in nature and a physical form that can convey this sublime. The art of India gets its inspiration from day-to-day life and it is the immediate experience of the dynamism that has been imparted in art. The joyous and effortless existence of life is here taken for granted; everything here is thin, light and obvious. Frankly, there is hardly any trace of spiritual quest. The unfounded love for little joys of life remained the keynote of this search; it is from this level that attempts were made to achieve the culminating state of all aesthetic enjoyment.

Throughout the ages, Indian art evinces a consistent growth, each succeeding phase starting with the heritage of the preceding one and leading the style to their natural and logical fulfilment. The material prosperity of Indian art had given birth to a class that was more open to sensuous delight. It must have facilitated the new form and fresh ideals to express beauty in art. There are faces and figures of human beings, which attract the beholders and invite admiration from them. They impress our sense-organs and lead us to an experience of ecstasy. The beauty comes in the form of a bliss, and the delight that we experience from a thing of beauty ultimately remains with us as a joy for ever.

Contents

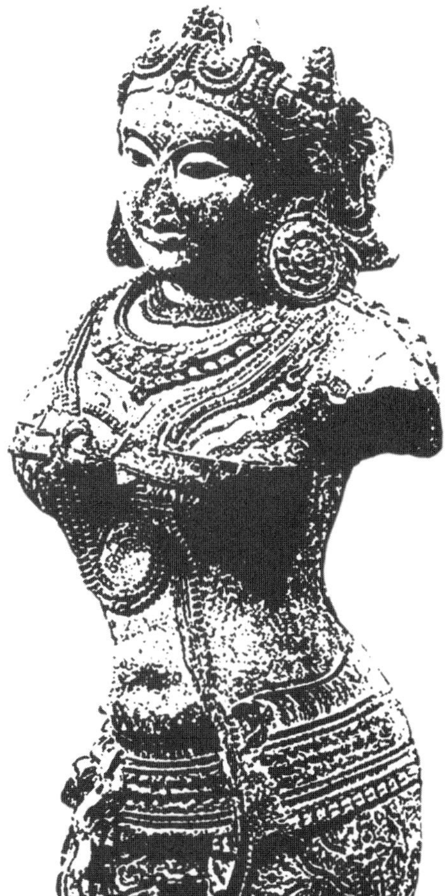

Acknowledgement

I am indebted to my spiritual teacher for his guidance for the collection of relevant materials for this volume, I am equally grateful to other scholars, whose published books and articles were consulted during the preparation of the manuscript of this volume and who supplied me unpublished and relevant information during discussions that contributed to the formation of my ideas.

I am grateful to Dr T.K. Biswas, Joint Director, Bharat Kala Bhawan, Banaras Hindu University, who went through the manuscript and forwarded invaluable suggestions. I am obliged to Prof. Deena Bandhu Pandey, Department of History of Arts, B.H.U., and all my colleagues of Bharat Kala Bhawan at Banaras Hindu University, who gave me encouragement in the preparation of this book.

I express my gratitude to the Indian Museum, Kolkata; National Museum, New Delhi; Patna Museum, Patna; State Museum, Gwalior; Bharat Kala Bhawan, Varanasi; Government Museum, Mathurā; and the Archaeological Survey of India, New Dehi

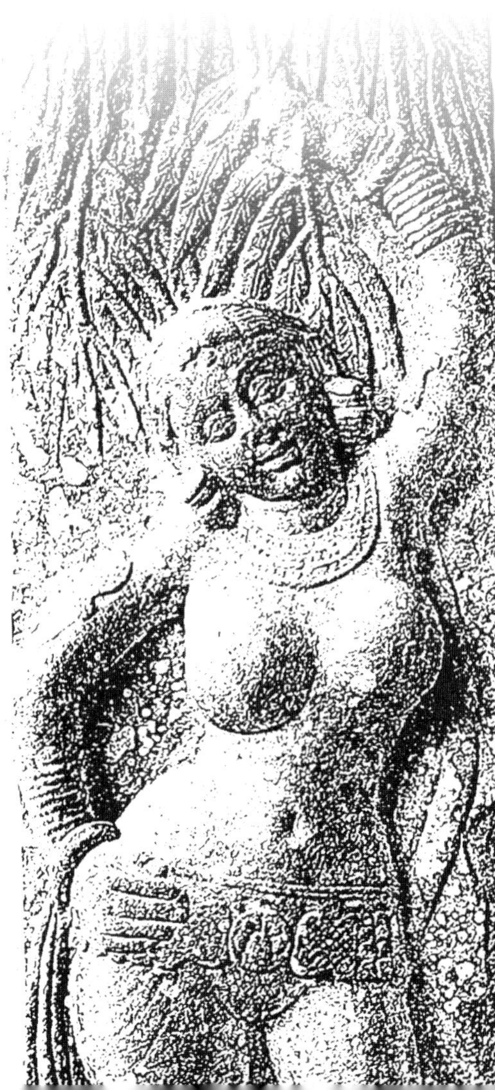

whose images have been used which were most essential to present the study. The volume wouldn't have been completed but for their courtesies.

I also wish to record my best wishes here for the moral support I received from time to time from my wife Vandana and my daughters Kavita, Pratima, Jyoti and my grandson Kartika (Gattu).

T.N. Mishra

List of Illustrations

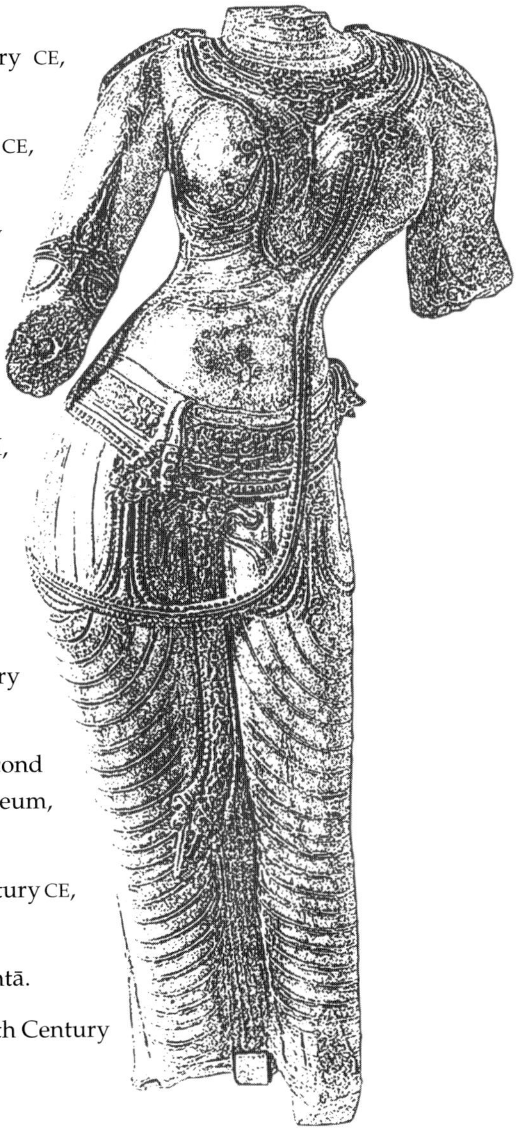

I

Introduction

THE culture of a nation is revealed through its tradition of art and literature. The culture partakes the look of a mosaic and is found composed of social manners and customs, religious beliefs and practices, parts and pastimes of every section of a society including the culture of the elites and of the common folk. This holds good with particular reference to India. Indian poets glorified every aspect of love and delved deep into ecstasies over the beauties of human body. The feelings for beauty and love guided the courses of Indian art throughout the ages.

The Upaniṣadic thinking believed that the ecstatic state of realization is only possible when a peaceful harmony between *ātmā* and

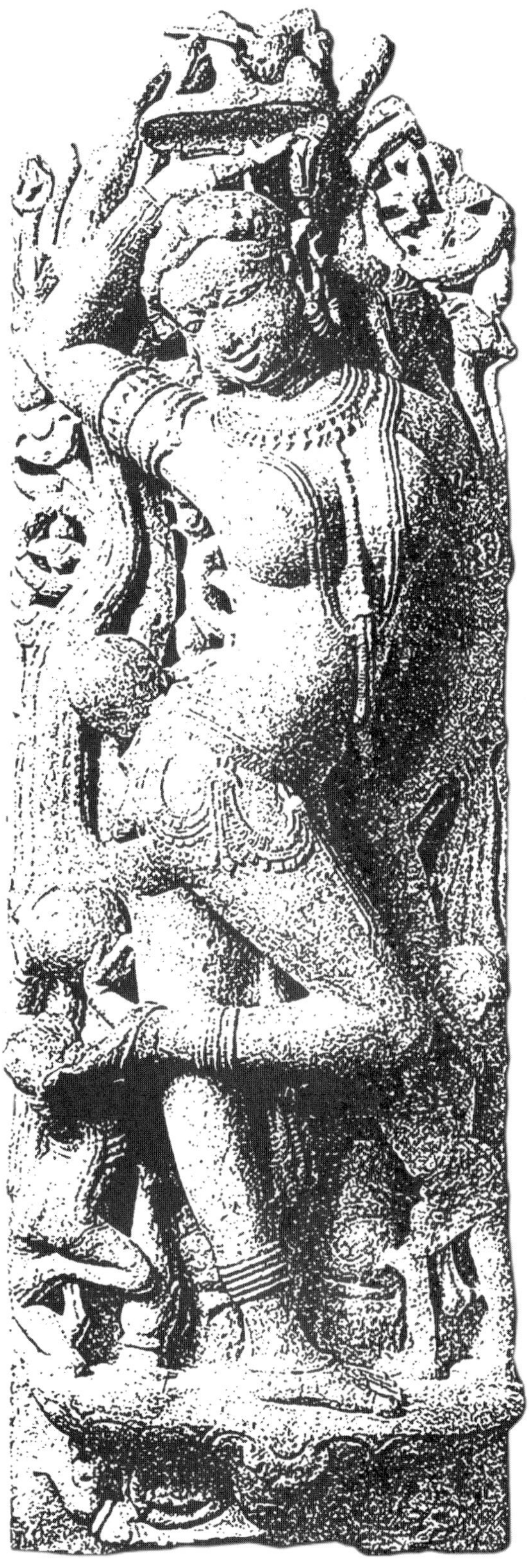

paramātmā is fully realized and in this state, one experiences the *rasa* or delight which is the same as *Brahma-svāda*. A peep into the past reveals that the tradition of Indian art started its journey from the days of pre-Indus period. This unique tradition thereafter continued in the art of Indus Valley regions. In this period, nature played a significant role in Indian art. The Vedic Indians not only lived in close proximity of nature but also did not fail in praising various forces of nature. They honoured such forces and began to worship them accordingly.

The period between fourth and first century BCE witnessed certain significant developments in the realization of art. A kind of atmosphere was created in which Formless Being was attributed a form (Icon). The period laid bare an evolution in which the deities were reflected initially in symbolic forms (both aniconic and theriomorphic) but later in anthropomorphic forms. Behind the anthropomorphic realizations (*pratimā*) of gods, there had been an intense action of devotion (*bhakti*). The word *bhakti* denotes complete surrender to one's beloved.

Devotion is essentially a kind of love — a love which is not merely the physical attraction. This is not an intellectual appreciation either. The abode of love is neither in the shape of a body or in the brain. It is to be found in the heart. Thus the nature of love cannot be understood by intellectual analysis or even by logical reasoning. The action of a pure love uplifts one above everything, above petty limitations.

Ancient Indian art had been a hand-maid of religion. The art of this phase is found to be intimately associated with Indian religion and philosophy. An icon (*pratimā*) did not only represent the form of a divine being but it also included subtle human moods and sentiments. Since the sculptor was himself a human being, for a case study, one may take the example of the Buddha's stone image in the Archaeological Museum at Sārnāth which is seen sealed in *dhamacakra pravartana-mudrā*.

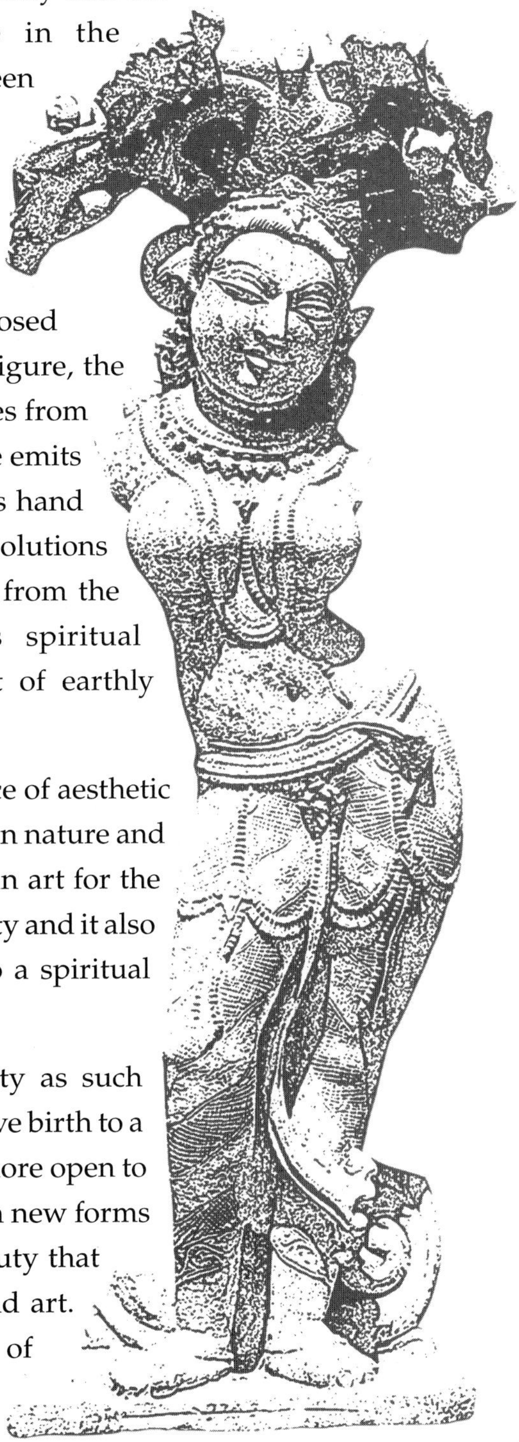

In this image, spiritually charged Lord Buddha is shown withdrawing from without and young within. To attain this concentration he fixed his glances of half closed eyes at the tip of his nose. To work out this figure, the unknown sculptor incorporated certain similes from nature (personification of nature) and his face emits an expression of compassion (*karuṇā*) and his hand gestures (*jñāna* and *vyākhyāna*) indicate his resolutions to eradicate the cause of sufferings (*duḥkha*) from the human mind. The image thus includes spiritual detachment and its concern for upliftment of earthly beings from the sentimental attachments.

The image just referred to is, in fact, a piece of aesthetic enjoyment since it combines in it the sublime in nature and a physical form which was the pivot of Indian art for the time being. It includes both dignity and nobility and it also indicates a flight from the material world to a spiritual world.

The material prosperity of Indian society as such during the initial centuries of Christian era gave birth to a class of people in the society which became more open to sensuous delights. This class opted for certain new forms in art and gave birth to a new diction of beauty that was expressed in contemporary literature and art. Sculptors and poets defined the concept of beauty nearly in the same language. To express the notion of beauty certain norms and canons were codified. Such norms and canons were exposed to alien influences, and changes in the thinking as well as in the practice of art were noticed. Male and female figures made in this period exhibited a feeling of cosmopolitanism. The sensuous figures that sculptors made not only commanded the admiration from the beholders but also excited their senses finally leaving an experience of ecstasy. Thus a piece of beauty turns as a source of delight and pleasure. This reminds of Kālidāsa who writes:

> Was she delineated in a picture and then endowed with life? Or she moulded in the creator's mind from the assemblage of lovely forms? When I meditate on the power of the creator and on her lineament, she appears to me like a match creation of the loveliest of women.

In *Mālavikāgnimitram*, the beauty is found described as how flawless, in every part, is her form! Her long eyes, her face lovely like moon of autumn, the arm sloping at the shoulders, her compact bosom with the plump and swelling breast, her sides as if polished, her waist measurable by this palm of the hand, her hips expansive, her feet with their curved toes, her body thus seems formed to suit the fancy of her teacher of dancing.

A careful analysis of both religions and secular subject matters in Indian art would show that visibly these are all engaged in the celebration of sensuous pleasures although the intent and purpose are essentially spiritual. The gods and goddesses are spiritual entities but when they are conceived in art they are fashioned with earthily sensuousness. Traditional Indian sculptors, modellers, painters always glorified the youth (*sadaiva taruṇaṁ vapuḥ*) and sensuousness pervaded most of the figure sculptures. The introduction of semi-nude females was made intentionally as it created more curiosity. Before the arrival of the Gupta period, the relieved narrative panels on religions exhibit that participants are engaged in celebrating life as such than to renounce it. Frankly erotic and passionate images, particularly of celestial nymphs (*yakṣīs*) and lovers in dalliance (*mithuna*) found carved on the religious structures played a pervasive role but the symbolic purposes of such images were generalized and were accepted in all the three religions.

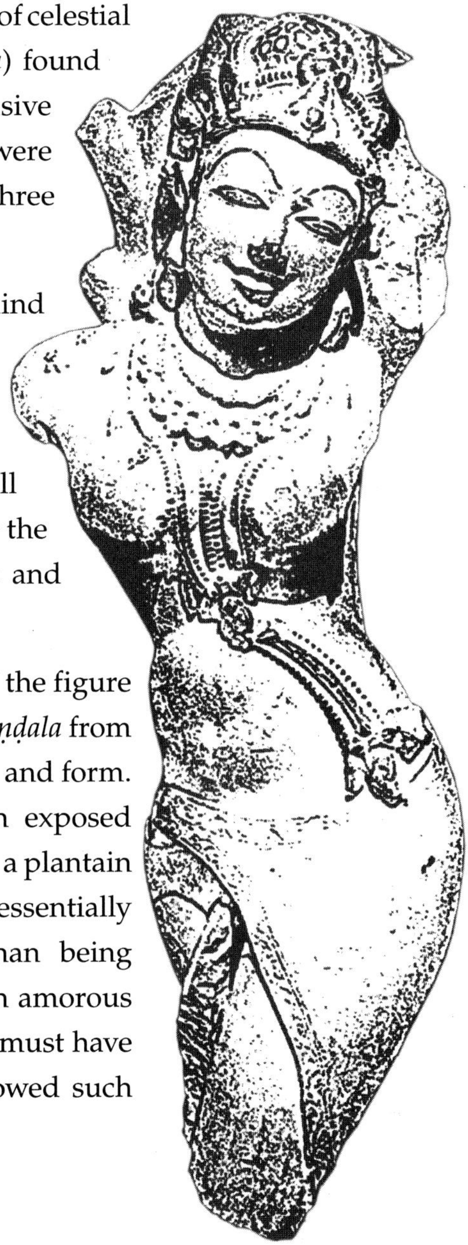

The disciplines, body and conquered mind appear to be the characteristics of the art of the Gupta period (fourth to sixth century CE). The relief sculptures of a little earlier date in Amarāvatī and Nāgārjunakoṇḍa revealed that all the dramatis personae are engaged in their life for the last time before entering a stage of detachment and discipline.

For example, a reference here may be made of the figure of *yakṣī* under a tree seen engaged in wearing a *kuṇḍala* from Amarāvatī which is quite conscious of her beauty and form. Another standing female from Amarāvatī with exposed thighs that call for a comparison with the trunk of a plantain tree. The thighs appears frankly naturalistic and essentially sensuous and therefore look more secular than being religious in its exposition. The exposition of such amorous motifs in religious architecture proves that there must have been something in the social climate which allowed such exposures in religious art.

Nature, from the very beginning, played a significant role in Indian art. In the classical phase in Indian art, certain similes in nature were personified and were incorporated in human forms to turn them more symbolic. Flowers and their petals served as the symbols of grace and beauty. In the early Buddhist narrative art, tree with young beauty, *śālabhañjikā* became a favourite subject matter. The intimate relation with women and tree motif was glorified in the art of Bharhut and Sāñcī (second-first century BCE). The worship of tree as goddess could be traced from the hoary part; same holds good with regard to the cult of fertility. It is interesting to note in all such activities that artists glorified young women only.

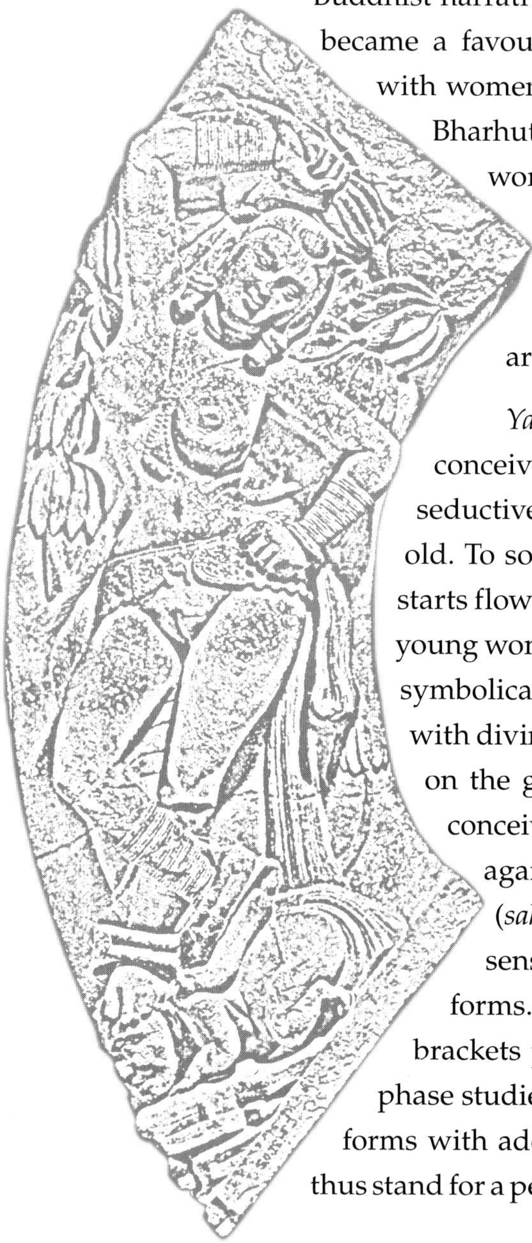

Yakṣī, vṛkṣakā, devatā, śālabhañjikā, etc. are all conceived as young women, sensuous and seductive. The notion of *śālabhañjikā* has been quite old. To some, it relates a fertility cult. A barren tree starts flowering or bearing fruit when it is kicked by a young woman or it is touched by a young lady. This is symbolically explained as representing soul's union with divinity. The *yakṣī* figures that serve as brackets on the gateways show a marked advancement in conceiving the plastic form of a young beauty against a tree either aśoka or a mango (*sahakārabhañjikā*). One finds the infusion of a sense of vitality in the figures of such female forms. Nearly nude, these females on Sāñcī brackets prove that the sculptors in the late Śuṅga phase studied perfectly and realized the young female forms with adept handling of the subject. Sāñcī females thus stand for a perfect union of spiritual and sensual aspects of the theme that runs like warp and weft of textile even in the succeeding phase.

The process of sensualization of religious figures once again come to the fore in the realization of the figure of goddess Śrī in ivory found from Ṭer (ancient Tagara) that dates back to second century CE. Goddess Śrī epitomizes abundance, fertility, blissful prosperity, luck and beauty. Keeping such qualities in goddess Śrī, the unknown ivory carver fashioned her. Her connection with the cult of fertility brings her nearer to the concept of *mithuna*. The ancient custom of fertility and virility came in the face of sexo-moral prosperity in the society and found its way in art to serve the cause of religion. Forms, once accepted, in art, have a tendency to become conventional and assume the character of a motif. The sap that runs through the bodies of trees is also found running in the entwining bodies of young females and the emotions and feelings in them thus become fully energized.

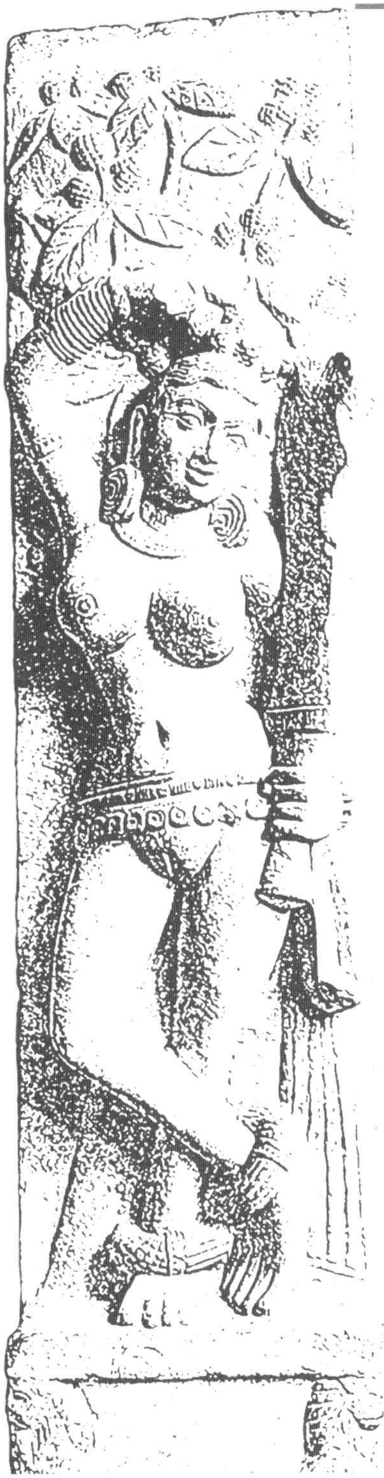

The passionate thrills with which young *yakṣīs* and *vr̥kṣakās* are charged, are also found continued in the young female forms in colour on the cave walls of Ajantā and Bāgh. The painting in the caves of Vākāṭaka-Gupta phase laid bare a kind of religious romanticism along lyric qualities in their female forms. The themes incorporate every aspect of life as such in the spiritual sense.

Above all, these arts are the visual record of a culture, the warm sensuous humanism, which found expression in art with utmost delicacy and beauty. They mirror their age and humanity and ideals which inspired them.

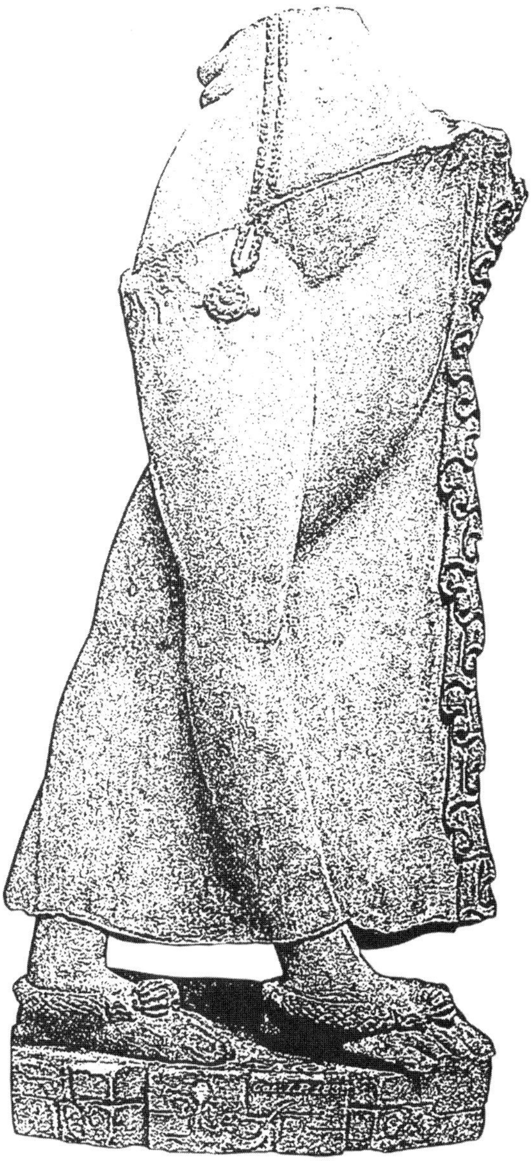

2

Feminine Beauty in Art

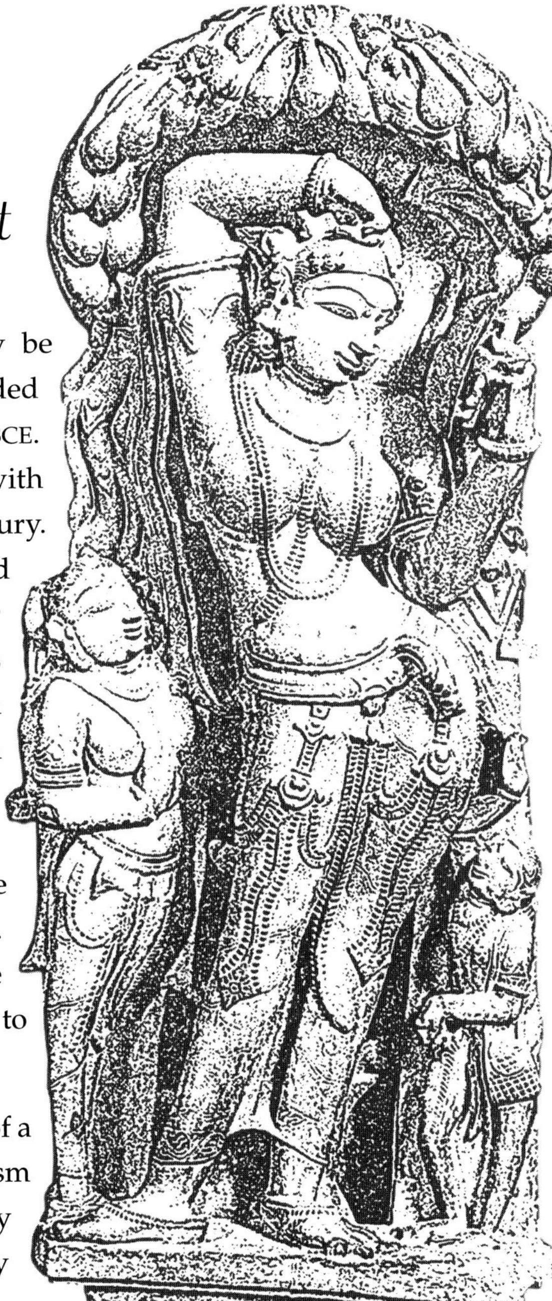

THE artistic heritage of India may be roughly said to have been handed down to her posterity from about 300 BCE. Ever since, this tradition continued with hardly any break till the present century. Though Indian art shaped, reshaped and had been moulded time and again under the influence of various socio-religious and cultural factors, yet its ultimate aim remains unchanged. Art's ultimate aim has always been the deliverance from the snare of illusion and attainment of the greatest delight (*ānanda*) through the experiences of truth and ultimate beauty. It is said that art conduces to fulfilling the aim of life, whose ultimate aim has been to attain final release (*mokṣa*).

The art maintains the visual record of a culture; the warm sensuous humanism generally finds its expression in poetry and, of course, in art of utmost delicacy and beauty. Both art and poetry mirror their age and humanity and such ideals which inspired them (Vaiṣṇavism and Sufism)[1] and kindled the creative enthusiasm of the age and preached the religion of love. The love they have in view, was not parental love of the father for his children, but love of lover for his beloved, a love that is most intimate, ecstatic and passionate. These are the universal feelings which are shared by human beings all over the world.

The history and culture of a nation is judged by its art and literature. It is also a mirror of the glory of the past as referred to by Daṇḍin: "Look! the image of fame of early king reflected in the mirror of the literature does not disappear even now in their absence."[2] Ancient Indian literature throws a mine of information about Indian art. The sculpture and painting of male and female (*nāyaka* and *nāyikā*) and the related poetry are remarkable for they incorporate romantic beauty, tenderness, unrestrained frankness and complete avoidance of sentimentality. In *Buddhacarita* Aśvaghoṣa supplements it as another damsel, holding the side of window and with her body flexed beautifully like a bow and look like a carved figure on the gateway.[3] Coomaraswamy also remarks that rarely has any other art combined so little fear with so much tenderness, so much delight with such complete renunciation. Indian art, at least, can teach us how not to misunderstand desire, we are constantly reminded here that the soul of sweet delight can never be defiled. Every art has a language. What words cannot express is sometimes conveyed in art through space enclosed in line and dabbed gesture. A vigorous rhythmical line is the basis of art.

The art attained a state of perfection in ancient India that could stand comparison with what was attained in other countries. Indian artist was not interested in originality and vigour in the handling of his subjects; he tried instead to remain true to the nature and in that direction he remained often unsurpassed. Throughout the ages, Indian art evinces a consistent growth in each succeeding phase starting with the heritage of the preceding one and leading the style to their natural and logical fulfilment.

The art of India is neither religious nor secular. Every aspect of life is incorporated into it and it also include values in the physical, psychological and metaphysical realms. In India, art is the form the artist impresses on a kind of formal life in Indian art; such a form results from performance. The work of art is also considered elsewhere as a ritual; according to Indian philosophy, through artistic activities an artist transforms himself. Form, ritual performance and transformation are inseparable aspects of Indian art. Indian artist sees this world with open mind and inner world with his closed eyes. So, he executes his work with ideas; twofold he visualizes the image, with direct intuition and his conscious vision which clothes it with the presence of God. God is the name, and work of art is body and house in which the formless or source of all forms reveals itself. This mode has two components, conceptual and formal. Conceptual thought defines, whereas visual thought embodies meaning. The continuity of life is carried by a stream of consciousness; such an action was embodied in the Indian sculpture as creative form in its

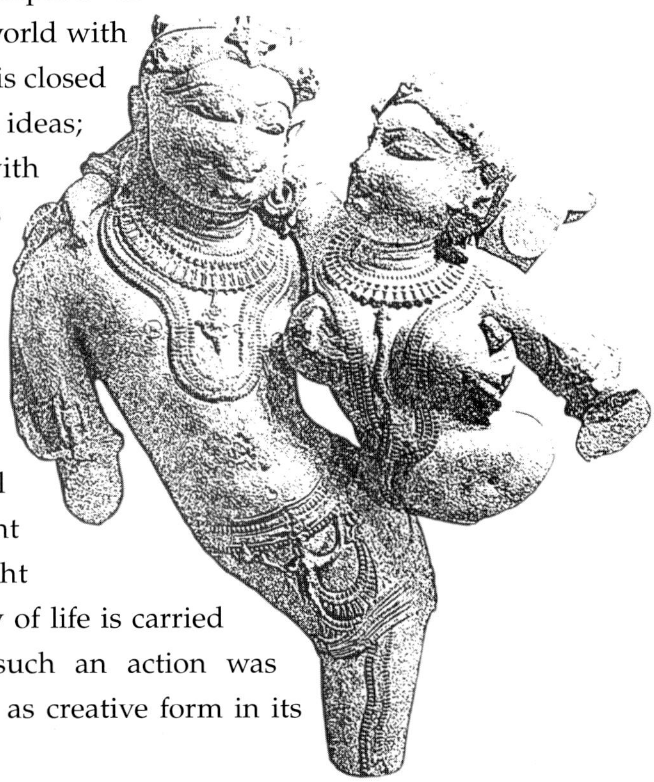

essence. Since it is in youth that this inner movement of life finds its fullest and most vital expression, it is invariably youthfulness in man and woman that captures the imagination and engrosses the vision of most of the artists of this period. The young human frame therefore shines in soft smoothness and in the transparent luminosity of its texture.

Indian art, in one sense, could be seen as a combination of the abstract philosophical concepts of Āryan origin and the representational, even naturalistic trends of Draviḍian. Indian art may also be described as theological and traditional. Tradition means a kind of healthy discipline conditioned by belief and prescriptions, which embrace the whole of civilization in all its modes and trends. Indian art, in all periods of development, was closely associated with the rhythm of life including the life of the gods and all living beings of earth. The Indian tradition interprets the living world as a manifestation of God. The symbols of art voice the same truth as our philosophy and myths. The tradition of art is handed down to us in the same framework as the verbal tradition; its realization put into the words by the sages at various times in the Indian literature. Once they are put into the words the timeless themes persist, and such themes are shaped in the tradition of the art by the adept hands of artist with skill, acumen and sensibility in his work. The artists were guided into a framework of time — which are being shaped and reshaped — ethnical heritage, cultural levels, etc., and regional conditions served as determining factors in this endeavour. It is an elementary and obvious truth that the particular form of any art is conditioned by the cosmic, psychological and metaphysical conceptions that lie at its base.

Art in its varied facts has been depicted through different mediums. Innumerable evidences of historical importance have been discovered through excavations and explorations of various monuments and sites in India, such discoveries thereafter received supports from a large amount of literary references. Ancient cultural heritage of India unfolds a glimpse of the past and thereby they laid bare the lifestyle of Indian people. This has been substantiated by written records. In all periods of development, art was closely associated with the rhythm of life of all living beings and Indian tradition interprets the living world as a manifestation of god.[4]

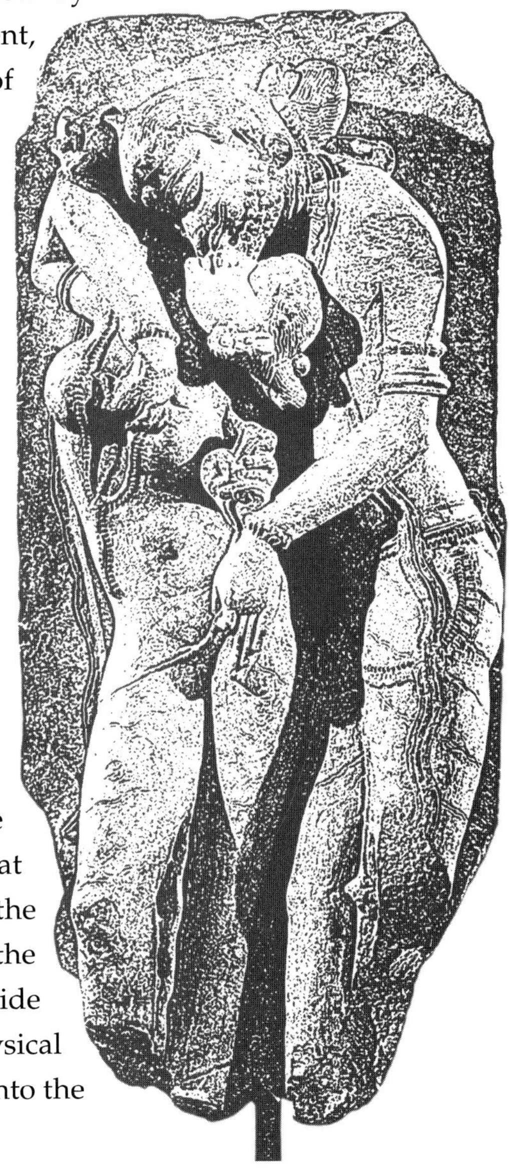

From third century BCE to the seventh century CE the Indian art had a common denominator, that is the faces and bodies of the figures formed a unity. The form of composition showed the consciousness of life. From the second century BCE and onward, the human figures and their movements seemed to carry them beyond themselves and their glances were full of meaning. Sculptural meaning flowed into posture and gesture, where creative consciousness is shown in the form of sculpture. The pivot of sculptural art is the human figure. It is the life of Indian people that causes the transformation in art. Thus the human figure itself becomes the conveyor of the unceasing flowing movement that used to reside in every youth. The face is lit up with physical discipline, mental wisdom and looking out into the visible world, where everything is at rest. It is youth that captures the imagination and engrosses the vision of the artist.

Basically this experience sprang from the notion of a disciplined body and a conquered mind which were sought to be achieved through centuries of conscious physical and intellectual efforts, known otherwise as the discipline of Yoga. Once the bodily discipline is achieved, there remains no scope for nervous tension of the body conditioned by emotions or suggestive of physical energy. This fact is not only found or seen in religious sculpture but also in ordinary mortals. Each figure, whatever be its position or action, exists by itself with deeper understanding of life. With the passage of time, the treatment becomes more delicate and sensitive and altogether a sensuous elegance results, till finally the outline seems to throb with an almost sensitiveness. All these show that they experienced bliss and joy of life.

The art of India gets its inspiration directly from the day-to-day life around, and it is the immediate experience of the dynamism and purposeful rhythm of daily life itself that has been imparted into this art. The joyous and effortless existence of life is here taken for granted; everything here is thin, light and obvious and frankly there is no trace of spiritual quest. The figure just bursts forth like flowers into light from the body. The unbounded love for the little joys of life remained the keynote of this search.

In the following lines, an attempt is being made to study the influence of sensualism and poetic touches in art. The term "sensuous" as used in work does not denote any fixed form. The nature and form of the motif vary according to the situation. The word sensuous is used here as expression of love; it covers the expression from the mild gesture of a lover putting his hand on the chin of the beloved to the extreme form as represented in the scenes showing an erotic act. The elementary sensuous representation finds its reflection in Indian art in the *mithuna* compositions. The word *mithuna*, ordinarily may mean nothing more than an amorous couple treated in proper artistic form, imagination and fancy of the sculptor who gave its full scope; this theme received loveliest commentaries of literary passages with an insight into the rich and glorious life of the best period of art in India. These aspects of the lovers described with such tenderness by Kālidāsa were graphically portrayed in many of the *mithuna* figures in early sculptures. The beautiful verses of Māgha describing the sport of a *dampati*, where the lover feels the body of the beloved are quite well-known.[5] This sensuous motif in sculptural art presents a variety of themes.[6] *Mithuna*, for instance, which appeared either in early Indian terracottas or on the *dvāra-śākhā*s of a Gupta temple appeared more as decorative appendage to Indian architecture, when translated into stone. The earliest depiction of *mithuna*s in lithic art is noticed on the art of the second century BCE; the monuments of Sāñcī and Bharhut exposed a number of such figures. The *mithuna* depiction on both these early monuments are mildly amorous. From the later half of the first century BCE, we see the beginning of the sensualization of *mithuna*. The depiction of the erotic motif from first century CE to third

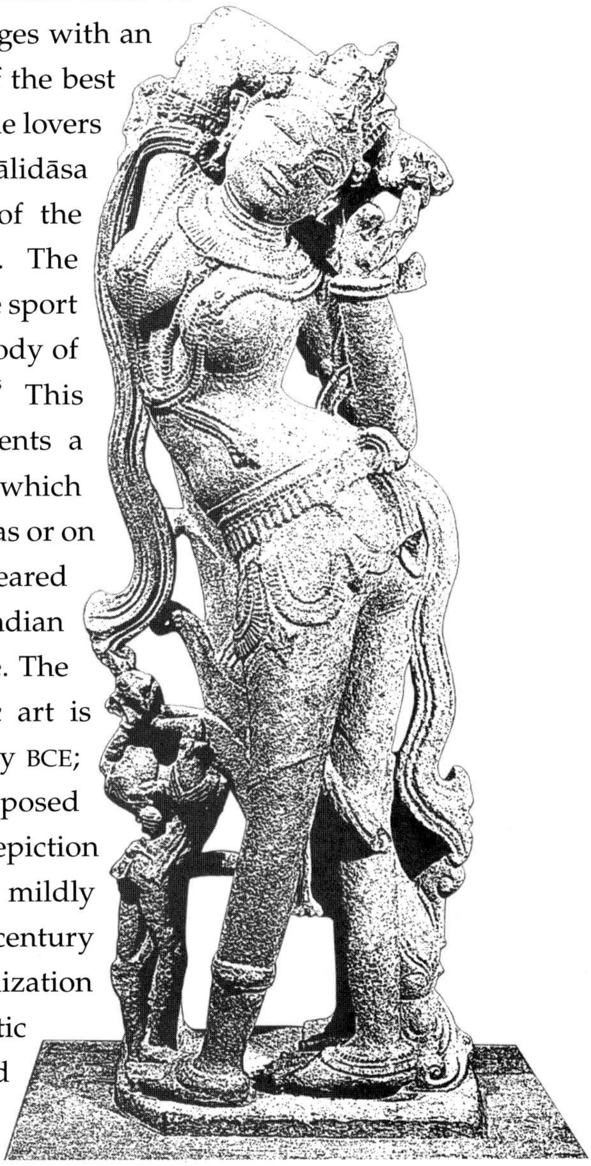

century CE was influenced by socio-cultural milieu of the period. Secular and sensual interests largely affected its portrayal, though its auspicious aspects were being retained. During the Kuṣāṇa period, the sensuous themes received more romantic touches in their depictions. These included a romantic pair in various amorous activities including embracing, kissing and other erotic activities. This is evident in the art of Mathurā, Karle and Nāgārjunakoṇḍa. Now the sculptors perhaps started favouring scenes depicting the *nāyaka-nāyikā bhāva* in various emotional states.[7] There must have been something in the social climate of the time that had encouraged the use of romanticism in the content and form, in embellishing the art. The consequent urban development in the early century of Christian era provided leisure and encouraged a taste for luxury. The luxurious life of cultural people (*nāgaraka*) and their taste in art led the way for the various artistic pursuits. These were the ideals to aspire and encouraged artists. Love is also treated as an art. Love is regarded as profound natural tenderness and solicitude, a serene joy based upon service and inter-flow between persons. It presumes perfect entente between the souls of the man and woman. The love which begins in the adoration of physical beauty develops into divine love, and all distinctions of sacred and profane disappear. This is the noble emotion which uplifts humanity and in whose glow we see the poetry and art in religion. It is this social climate that seems to have had inspired Vātsyāyana to compile his *Kāmasūtra*, the masterly textbook on love into fourfold Hindu scheme of life and this text served as the guidance of cultured married couples. The Bāṇa's literature unfolds on the other hand a picture of the life of *nāgaraka* and courtiers, who used to meet occasionally for cultural discussions. The lifestyle of a *nāgaraka* became a favourite theme in the plays of Bhāsa and Śūdraka, who flourished at this time. It is this sensual sentiment in men and women that ultimately led to the use of sensuousness in art and literature. Undoubtedly, this common theme was treated with individualistic approaches in poems and paintings of the period and the rich, expensive feudal empire became a kind of kaleidoscope, which reveals the loveliest flowers in its turnings, and one finds at once the wonder and delight in contemplating the haunting, tender beauties.

Emotions (*bhāva*) are the powerful means of moving a recipient through and through and provides thereby a unique and detached delight (*rasa*). The artists and poets are able to exchange the emotional experiences with their recipients and thus establish a mutual link between them through their artistic activities while Indian art be it secular or religious reflects an ambivalence that appears as a celebration of the sensuous even though the intent is spiritual. The gods and goddesses are spiritual entities but their forms are often sensuous, if not erotic. Youthfulness is also regarded as an essential feature, and indeed, this is more true in case of Indian goddesses. The glorification of youth and sensuousness remained pivotal in early Indian sculptures. The semi-nude forms of the female were carved in such a way that they appeared to celebrate life with all its glories than to renounce. The frank eroticisms of some images, particularly *yakṣī*s (celestial nymphs) and *mithuna* (lovers in dalliance), play a pervasive role in embellishing the sculptural art. In this light, if we see at a glance, the sculptures leave no doubt that the Indian artists were quite successful in expressing this ambivalence.

The documentation of secularization and sensualization

is clearly noticeable in *stūpa* architecture and, in particular, in the reliefs adoring *stūpa*s at Amarāvatī and Nāgārjunakoṇḍa. In these two centres of Andhra School, was emphasized depiction of such scenes in the life of the Buddha that are related prior to his enlightenment, specially, his life before abandoning *saṁsāra* (world) including the luxurious life he led in his harem and in the court, etc. The depictions are more sensuous than religious and far less Buddhistic. It does not speak of, nor aim at, suggesting the Buddhist ideal of renunciation or *nirvāṇa* or discipline and the strict ethical virtues including avoidance of woman. The relief sculptures of these centres appear frankly naturalistic and essentially sensuous. The disciplined body and conquered mind happen to have been the characteristics of art of the Gupta period. The relief-sculptures of Amarāvatī and particularly, of Nāgārjunakoṇḍa, revealed all the dramatis personae as seemingly engaged in enjoying their life, for the last time, before entering into a stage of detachment and discipline of the succeeding period. The treatment rendered in art of these places appear artistic and poetic. It is interesting to note that a number of amorous figures were adjusted just next to the Buddhist scenes. There must have been something in social climate of the time that encouraged the use of erotic motifs as a form of an embellishment in religious art. The idea was, perhaps, to indicate the impermanence of physical beauty and the futilities of worldly attachments. The quest was for the ultimate truth, the ultimate beauty.

The secular subjects drawn from everyday life were introduced in the art of historic period. The fertility cult was accepted in religious theme and was given an artistic treatment in such a way that it turned out into an art motif. The process of secularization and sensualization of ritual and cultic objects is clearly noticeable in the ivory figure of Śrī — goddess of abundance, fertility, blissful prosperity, luck and beauty found at Ṭer (ancient Tagara), that has been assigned to the second century CE. The cult of fertility (specially, the cult of goddess Śrī) has a direct bearing on the depiction of *mithuna*s in religious art. The ancient customs or rituals meant for the community and the fertility and virility came in the face of evolved sexo-moral prosperity in the society and found their way to art representations in the service of religion.

This is the urge of the spirit in us, the spirit that is emancipated and free. The self attains its perfection when it is able to reach the ideals of true knowledge, morality and creation of aesthetic excellence. While knowledge gives a vision of life to the artist and reveals the meanings and secrets of many events, the moral attitude gives a direction and content to the artistic creations. There are relief faces and figures of human beings which attract the beholders and invite admiration from them. They impress our sense-organs and lead us to an experience of ecstasy. We rarely come across a human being who is not happy to see a beautiful face and figure; the beauty comes in the form of an enjoyment and delight that we experience, whenever we have a contact with such things.[8]

In the paintings of Ajantā and Bāgh, the figures involved in dance and music and in the festivals of love seemingly look like dark aboriginals, specially in the large dance panel on the façade of the Bāgh caves. The rhythmic splendour of many other scenes in both the cave complexes derives from the sap that runs through nature. The thrills of burning passion are seen everywhere on the walls to inspire human emotion and feelings. The feelings of the youth burst in the act of love with abandon. All the Jātaka myths become blurred in the fresh freedom of prevalence of youthful pleasure-loving couples. In the art expression at this place, one finds a complete statement of indivisible union of the sacred and secular art. In the Ajantā wall paintings one feels definite departure from the art of early Buddhism, where emphasis was more on symbolic expression, keeping, thereby, one away from the world of reality. Ajantā paintings laid bare a kind of religious romanticism imbued with lyric

fig. 1. Ajantā painting, Fifth Century CE, Ajantā.

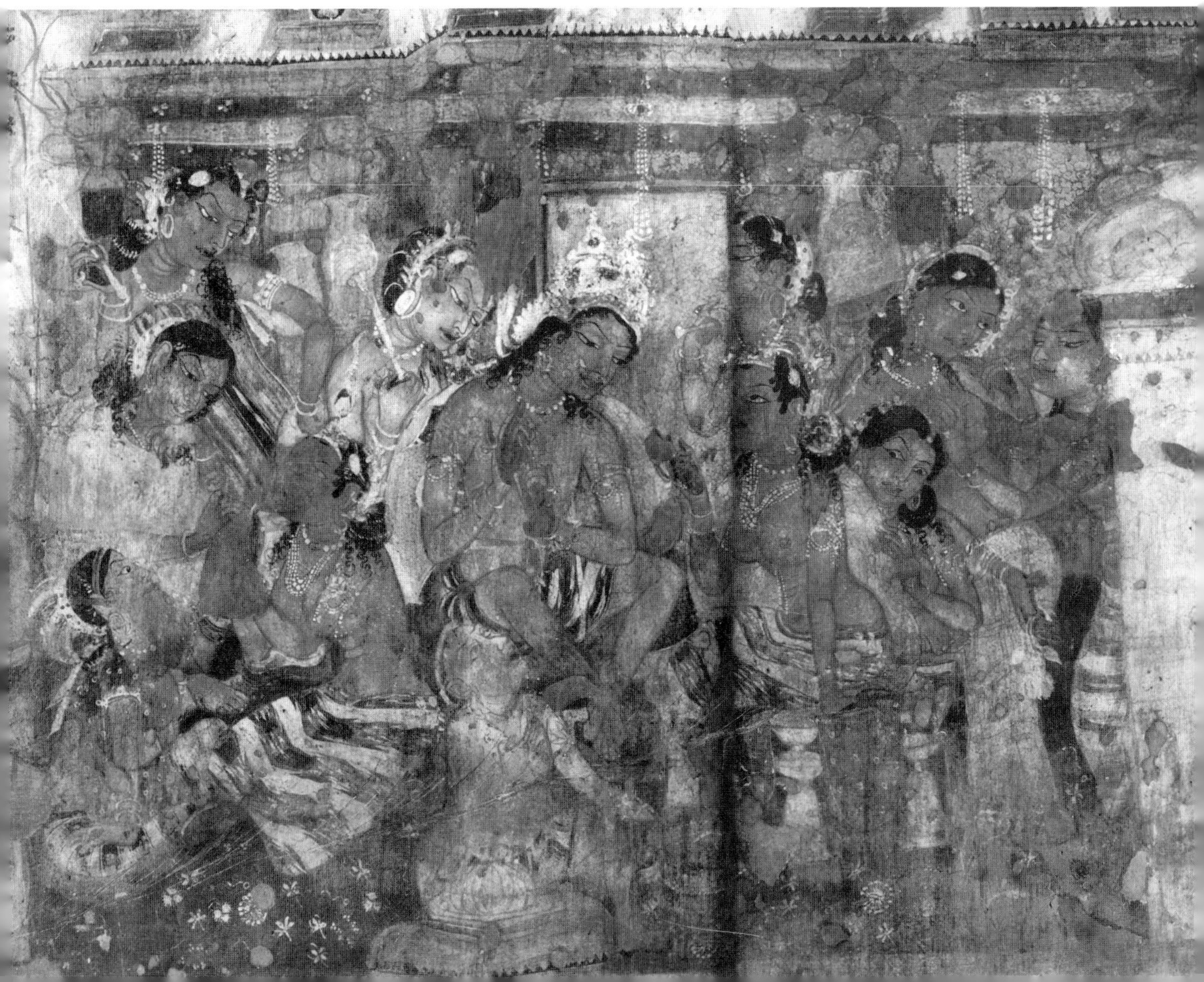

quality, a reflection encompassing every aspect of life as such in the spiritual sense, and as an aspect of the divine. Sensuous physical beauty becomes here an emblem of spiritual beauty. Hence, it reminds that life had become an art, but the ultimate goal of it was never forgotten.

The art of India as well as the religion and culture absorbed several foreign traits from certain Central Asian nomadic tribes including the Śakas and Kuṣāṇas who reached India in the first century BCE and ruled over the northern part of India, including Pāṭaliputra. The depiction of the erotic motifs and sensuous physical beauty in Indian art during this period was considerably influenced by the socio-cultural milieu of the period. The secular and sensual interests largely affected their portrayal through this social mutation. Yet, some of its earlier aspects were retained. Erotic and sensuous themes of this period visibly received more romantic touches in their depictions. Sensual and worldly interests were clearly betrayed in full bodied and enticing figures of *yakṣīs* or female figures on the railings of the Mathurā. An important development during the early third century CE was traced in the representation of the couple and other erotic themes on the doors and entrances of the monuments. The available *mithuna* motifs of the period underwent major changes including the deeper sensualization of the motifs as such. The profuse use of the *mithuna* motifs in art with the increasing number and with a greater sense of depth in sculptures paved the way for advancement in the artist's understanding of human figures. The increasing interest in the depiction of avidly sensuous forms suggests that, by this time, *mithuna* motif became a socially acceptable form of decoration and reflected the cosmopolitan culture of urban Mathurā.

The consequent urban development in the early centuries of the era seems to have encouraged a taste for offering more voluptuousness in art. Erotic depictions were permitted in religious arts because it was considered auspicious. The Indian aesthetic traditions maintained close relationship between the visual and performing arts particularly dance and drama.[9] The profuse carvings of erotic scenes that begin in the Gupta and post-Gupta-early Cālukyan temples were not to excite the sensual feelings of the onlookers but to inform them of the divine presence in these very situations where we are most likely to forget them. The emphasis on human impulse, which appeared in terracotta plaques of the temple at Bhītargāon, made the sensuous appeal of the *mithuna* couples an essential part of contemporary iconography. The sculptures and paintings in the cave of Ajantā and Ellorā are supposed to be the wonders of art. Take away these religious aspects from these arts, and see the difficulty in interpretation of remaining subject matters. How can one understand the relevance and significance of certain postures, facial expressions and other symbols used in these arts without correlating them with the spiritual background which inspired them and formulated the form and content of art? The sculptures acquired a different quality and the artists took care to express the figural beauty and poise of the male and female postures in such sculptures and paintings and also displayed in them a typical charm, which is known as *lāvaṇya* that granted a unique aesthetic surface in them. All important religious sects of the country presented sensuous and erotic motifs in their art. Sensuous representation in art was a pan-Indian cultural feature. It implies a common cultural substratum which influenced religious sects all over India. This common substratum is seen in those beliefs and practices which show the primal connection between sex and religion. Far from being suppressed, sex played an important part in the religious life of early communities and civilizations. It was realized and felt necessary to carry certain experiments in art before conventionalizing the aspects in text like the *śilpa*-canons. Forms, once accepted in art, have a tendency to become conventionalized and assume the character of motifs. In the culture of India which glorifies traditional values, the processes of conventionalizing become a major factor leading to persistence and inertia in the use of motifs.

The religious structures were the means to express the above-mentioned philosophy and motifs. The subjects drawn from everyday life were introduced in religious art and architecture also. It must be remembered that every work of Indian art and architecture must, first and foremost, be regarded from the point of view of its metaphysical aspect, a kind of replica of some unseen region of which the metaphysical factor determined the plan and elevation. The sculptural decoration of the temples points the way to that desired union; this meaning is implicit in the multiple representations of *mithuna* in erotic embrace, the ultimate union of the soul with the divine. These happy couples, intensely interested in one another and admiring each other with such warmth are eloquent symbols of love; that noble emotion uplifts humanity from the animal level, and in whose glow we see the birth of true art and of religion as well. We did not distinguish between sensuousness and spirituality. One leads into other, and we see at once the spiritual in the sensuous.

The habitual preaching of generation after generation of

learned men left a substratum of metaphysical awareness that found expression in mundane literature and art of the Gupta period, in fourth century. So complete is the hold of this transcendentalism that what was then called *kalā* (art) is throughout reflective, at one move or another, of this philosophy of the life process. From the fifth century CE and onwards, there was a change in the political scenario which influenced the socio-economic pattern of life. Another significant development was the rise of Tantrism. Magical beliefs and practices acquired great importance under Tāntric cults. From the fifth century onwards we get inscriptional evidences of Tāntric worship. Belief in Tantra became a significant factor that influenced the erotic art of the period.

The depiction of erotic motifs in art had a long tradition from the remote past and the relationship of Tantrism to sexual depiction has to be viewed in historical perspective. The *mithuna* (amorous couple) has been traditionally accepted in Indian art as an auspicious symbol since the beginning of the historical period. In the so-called Daśāvatāra temple at Deogarh, built at about fifth century CE, *mithuna*s were found carved on the plinth. This seems to suggest the flexibility in the placement of erotic motifs. In the sixth century CE, the depiction of *mithuna* was introduced, for the first time, in the temple architecture of Aihole, Paṭṭaḍakala, Bādāmī and Mahākūṭeśvara. Their presence was on the door-point and their inclusion was along with other auspicious decorations. Seemingly, such depiction in the *dvāraśākhā* appear to have had a magico-religious function. These sculptures in highly amorous poses indicate that priests and devotees, at this time, did not object to their presence on the religious edifices. By this time, the temples were recognized as important socio-religious centres and provided opportunities for the development of arts. The cave of Bādāmī profusely laid bare the presence of a sizeable number of erotic motifs. Sensuous compositions with poetic touches are clearly seen in the bas-reliefs over all the pillars and pilasters, in the rear wall of the veranadah as well as in the *maṇḍapa*, lintels and ceilings, etc. Erotic motifs can also be seen in the cave-arts of Ajantā and Ellorā. Ajantā paintings offered a sort of religious romanticism imbued with lyric quality, a reflection encompassing every aspect of life, as such, in the spiritual sense, and are considered as divine. But even in this splendorous art, which exalts all human emotions and feelings, we are made to feel the evanescence of the phenomenal world. The amorous scenes which appear to bring the ineffable luxury of the dark sensuous bodies burning with passion before one's eyes, were mocking at all mysteries beyond that of the moment. Sensuous physical beauty became an emblem of spiritual beauty and the nude figure and *mithuna* scenes are found carved in an inconspicuous corner of certain temples such as Paraśurāmeśvara temple of Bhubaneshwar, Kailāsanātha temple of Ellorā and the Someśvara temple of Mukhaliṅgam.[10] The period reveals a contrast in the treatment of *mithuna* and *maithuna* themes; the former was accepted as convention, and the latter had to make way due to prescriptions of the *Śilpaśāstra*s.

The temple of Khajurāho confronts us with the acknowledgement of Vātsyāyana's gospel of the happy life. The structures show that sculpture and architecture had become one. Some of the panels in the Kandarīya and Lakṣmaṇa temples, have also become part of the repertory of the most sensitively chiselled world of sculpture. Apart from the whole conception of each temple as representing the ethos of sensuous appeal, the various creative energies became image in fluid mood, wrought as finely as the imaginative skill of the artisans can make stone fluid.

The Pārśvanātha, Ādinātha and Duladeva temples were built at the end of the eleventh century; the Duladeva seems to be dominated by Śaiva cult, and the female figure on the bracket reaches here the acme of virtuosity in the carving of alluring flying females. In the monumental sun temple at Koṇārka, orchestration of the harmony of the moods of love finds expression on a grandeur scale. The dominant faith in the sun, as the source of energy, is further reflected in the carvings of its giant figures. These new interpretations suited the prevailing environment and hardly disturbed the form and structure of art in degrees. There are lovely faces of women like moon of autumn, having heavy breasts; such qualities characterize those who play the musical instruments on the upper storey of the

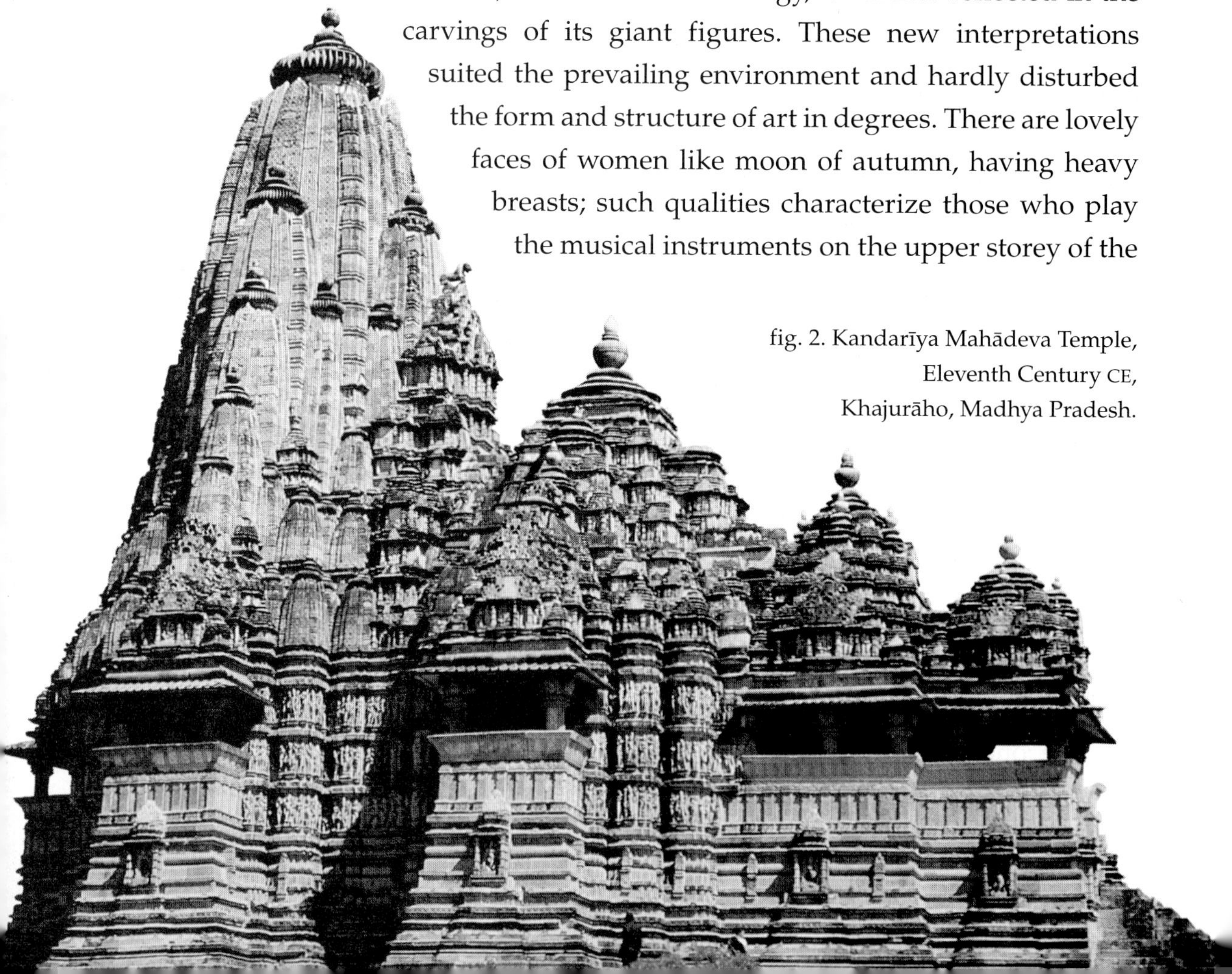

fig. 2. Kandarīya Mahādeva Temple, Eleventh Century CE, Khajurāho, Madhya Pradesh.

Jagamohana; the relief lovers on the wall are also noteworthy. One of the great sculptures of all time shows a kissing couple in Koṇārka verily engaged in a passionate embrace. When such an ideal is achieved in the embrace of his beloved, a man forgets the whole world — everything, both within and without — and enjoys greatest joy, *ānanda*. There the expression retains a certain ambivalence; it has more charm than mystery. The face of the image registers the reflex of psychological expression and the glance of it shows that it is absolutely within itself. No doubt, India presents the scene of a cultural milieu in which all the divergent elements have been brought together to form a common pattern for the purpose of artistic expression of their ideas and thoughts. The religious architecture from the eight to ninth century onwards provided opportunities for the exhibition of artistic talents and the power of wealth. The temple architecture and the icon of the God and the related themes became chief concern for the artists and their patrons. Superstition and belief in magic held sway over such people and, at the same time, the regional sentiments influenced the cultural pursuits. The atmosphere around the medieval temple was breeding ground for luxurious living and degenerated sexual practices. Curiously

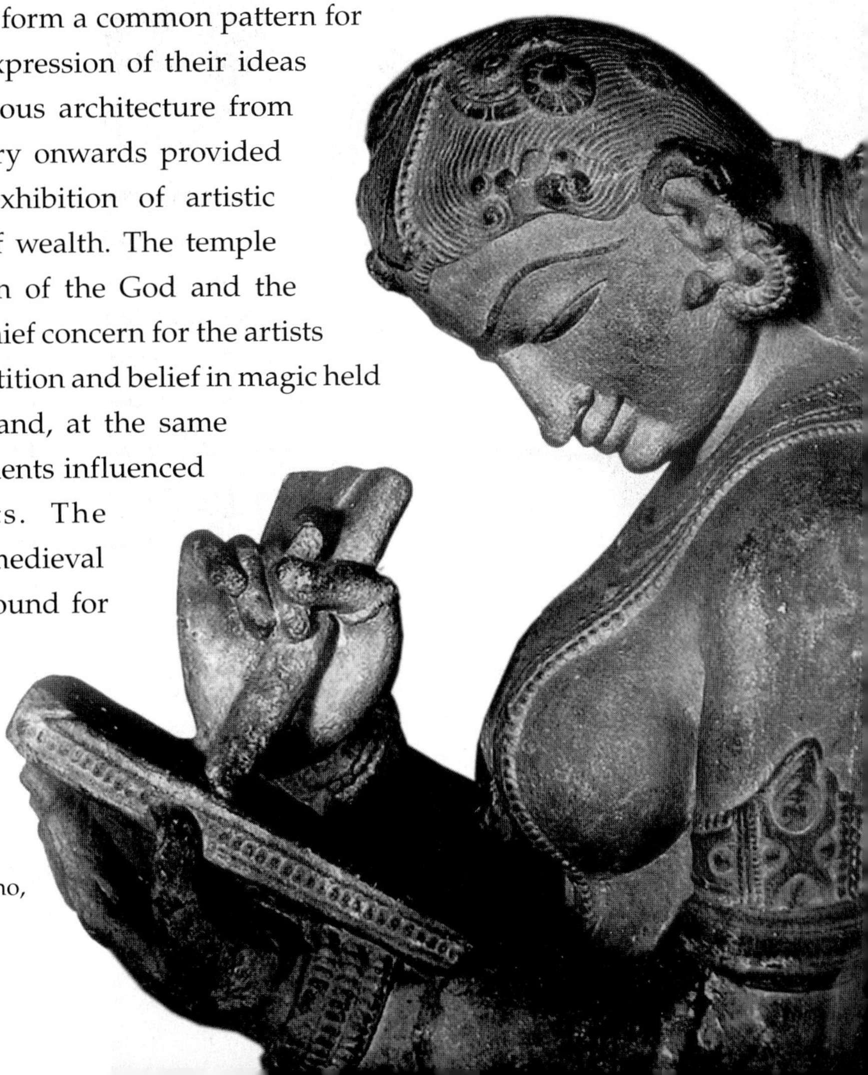

fig. 3. Writing a letter, Stone, Eleventh Century CE, Khajurāho, Indian Museum, Kolkata.

enough, in spite of the passage of the time, the classical tradition of Indian art was still being maintained in places. The erotic motifs experienced regional variations. The attitude towards erotic realization in art appeared different in each region. Eroticism, as an auspicious motif, appears to have been accepted in art of the period. The presence of such compositions seems to have fulfilled some particular functions; they probably suggest the prevalence of some strong beliefs and are not necessarily connected with any religious sects.

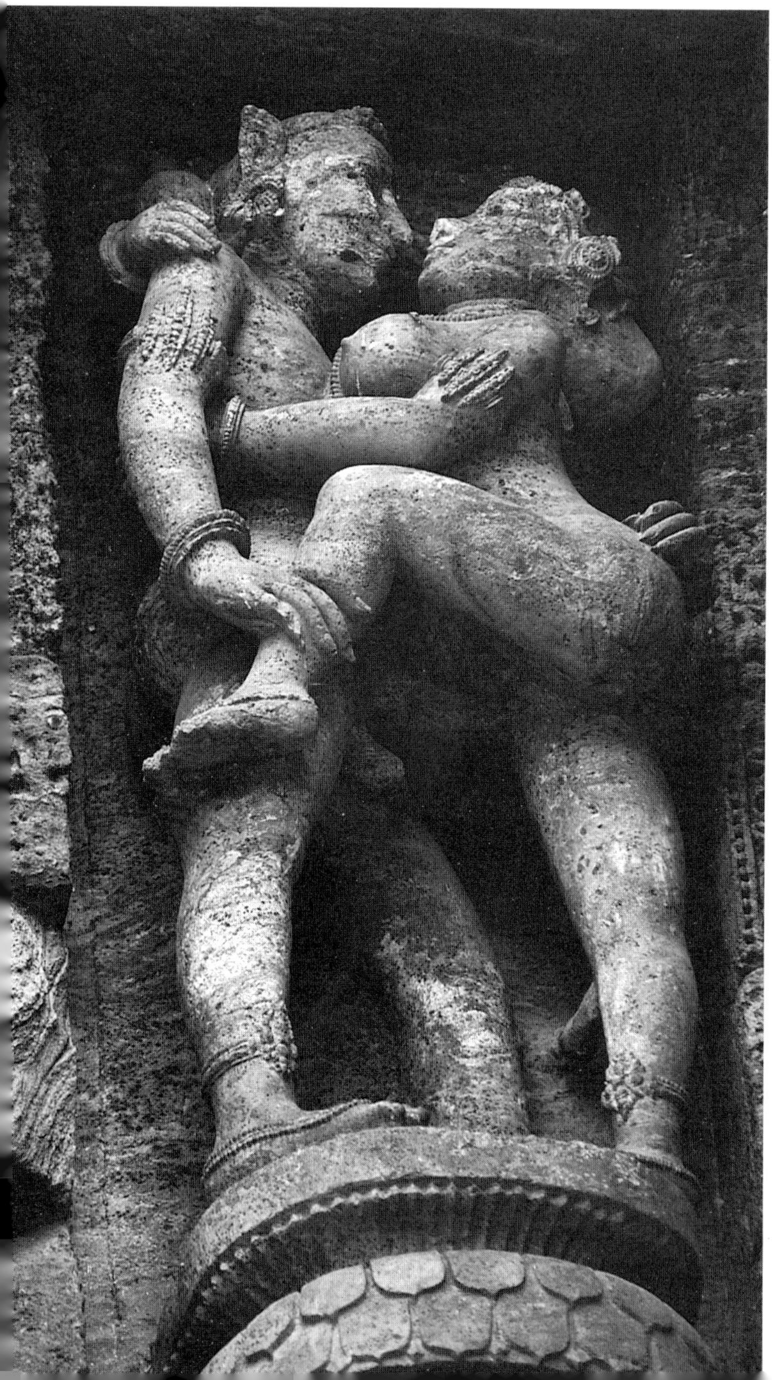

So much ado has been made about the frank eroticism of the sculptures of religious shrines that, perhaps, now is the time for a valid observation and a fresh review. A creative sensuousness has always been regarded as an important source of energy, of vital urge in life, as much in religious and spiritual

fig. 4. *Mithuna* (erotic couple), Stone, Eleventh Century CE, Khajurāho, Madhya Pradesh.

quest as in the quest for expression, and the *mithuna* and *maithuna* idea in sculptural art finds the most creative expression. Indeed, it was accepted as a normal and essential expression of life, without any shame and secrecy attached to it, as indicated in the temple of Purī and Koṇārka, where admittedly the eroticism is not only in the sensuous suggestiveness but the sexual act included in a wide variety of poses and attitudes. Perhaps, the artist got the inspiration from Vātsyāyana's *Kāmasūtra* which appears to have influenced the art of the period and no creative imagination remained unaffected by the tenderness brought to the human relations. Certainly, the odour and sweat of sex is made sacred, and no shame is attached to it. The habitual preachings, generation after generation, of learned men; left as a substratum of metaphysical awareness, offers immortality in that realm where there are joys and delights, enjoyment combined with felicity and extreme fulfilment of the desire of *kāma*.[11] This blissful condition comes to be epitomized in the word *ānanda* and in Upaniṣads the essence of all human knowledge is comprehended under this concept, identified with the Ultimate Reality.

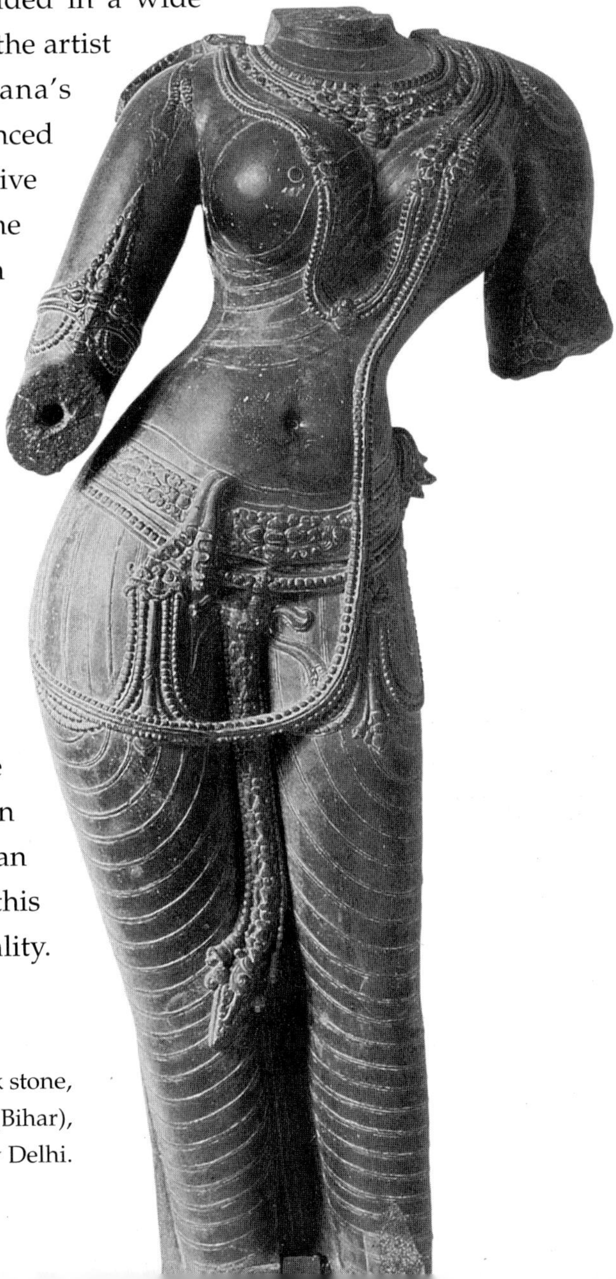

fig. 5. Tārā, Black stone, Eleventh Century CE, Nālandā (Bihar), National Museum, New Delhi.

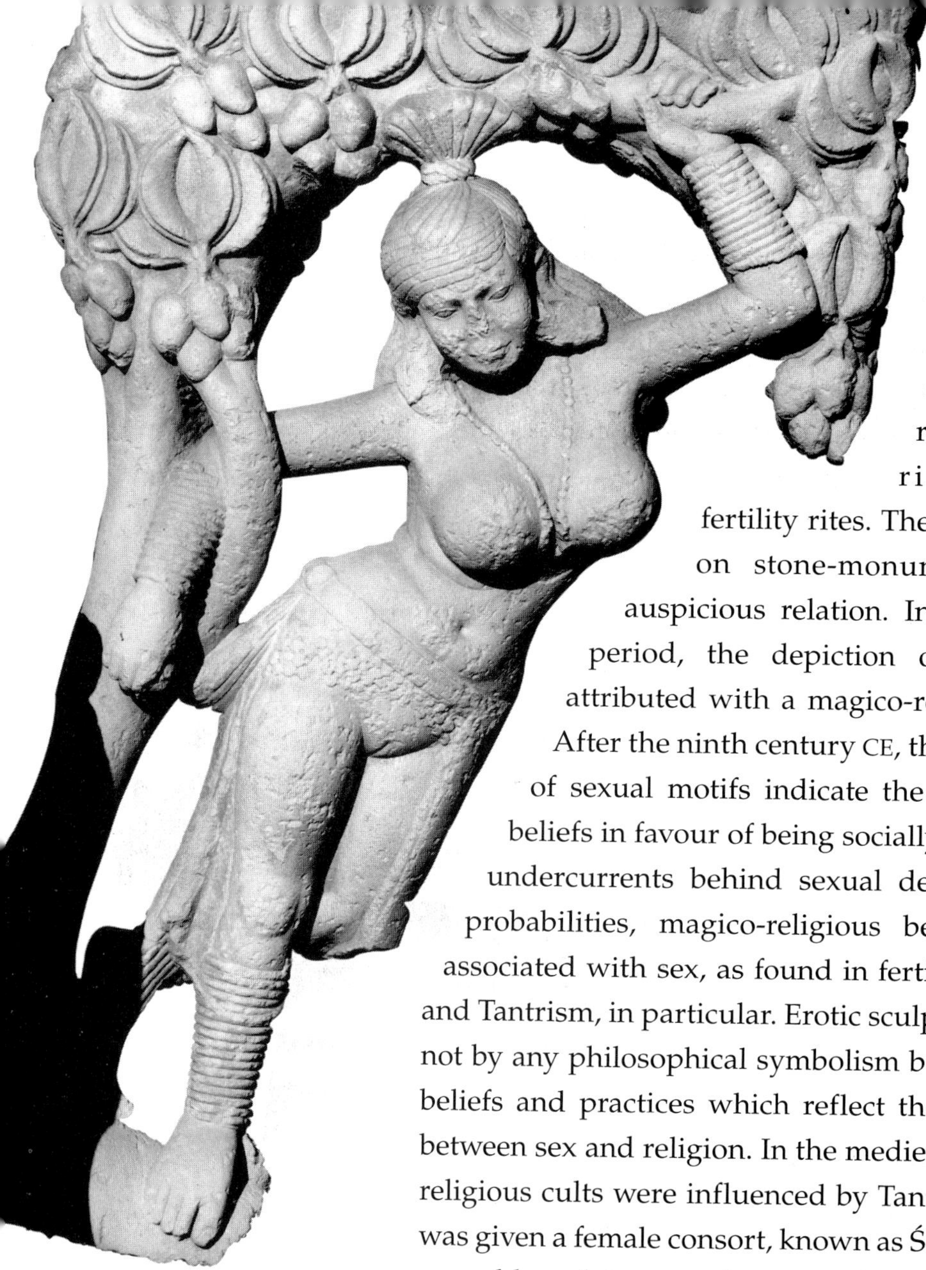

The depiction of couples in terracotta art is considered by some as the representative of the ritualistic pair in fertility rites. The portrayal of couples on stone-monuments indicates an auspicious relation. In the early medieval period, the depiction of erotic pairs was attributed with a magico-religious significance. After the ninth century CE, the general acceptance of sexual motifs indicate the prevalence of some beliefs in favour of being socially accepted. The basic undercurrents behind sexual depiction were, in all probabilities, magico-religious beliefs and practices associated with sex, as found in fertility rites, in general, and Tantrism, in particular. Erotic sculptures are influenced not by any philosophical symbolism but by those religious beliefs and practices which reflect the primal connection between sex and religion. In the medieval period, nearly all religious cults were influenced by Tantrism and every god was given a female consort, known as Śakti. They addressed a goddess by general term of "Bhagavatī." Religious literature and belief give impetus to the worship of gods with their consorts which is also found reflected in medieval iconography. Temple of Bhubaneshwar, Khajurāho, Kadwana, Nāgdā, Belūr, Halebiḍ, Somanāthapura and

fig. 6. Tree and Women, Sandstone,
East toraṇa of Stūpa I, First Century BC,
Sāñcī, Madhya Pradesh.

Ambarnāth have representations of deities in pair and, at times, in amorous attitudes along with their Śaktis. May be, some religious system was the major factor in bringing about the spiritual transformation in the depiction of *mithuna*. The change in depiction was due to social permissiveness and due to influence of Tantra.[12] This is also found in literary works including poems dealing with religious themes which were endowed with sensuality[13] and worldly consciousness that is seen in temple sculptures where there is nothing spiritual in expression or association. However, the attributes of prosperity, fruitfulness and fertility are still associated with erotic motifs. The cultic function was associated with this notion and then superseded by aesthetic and sensual feelings.

References

1. Vaiṣṇava and Sufi did not distinguish between sensuousness and spirituality. One leads into other, and we see at once the spiritual in the sensuous.

2. आदिराज यशोम्बिमादर्शं प्राप्य वाङ्गमयम् ।
   तेषाम् सन्निधानेपि पश्य नाद्यपि नश्यति ॥

   ādirāja yaśombimādarśaṁ
   prāpya vāṅgamayam ।
   teṣām sannidhānepi
   paśya nādyapi naśyati ॥

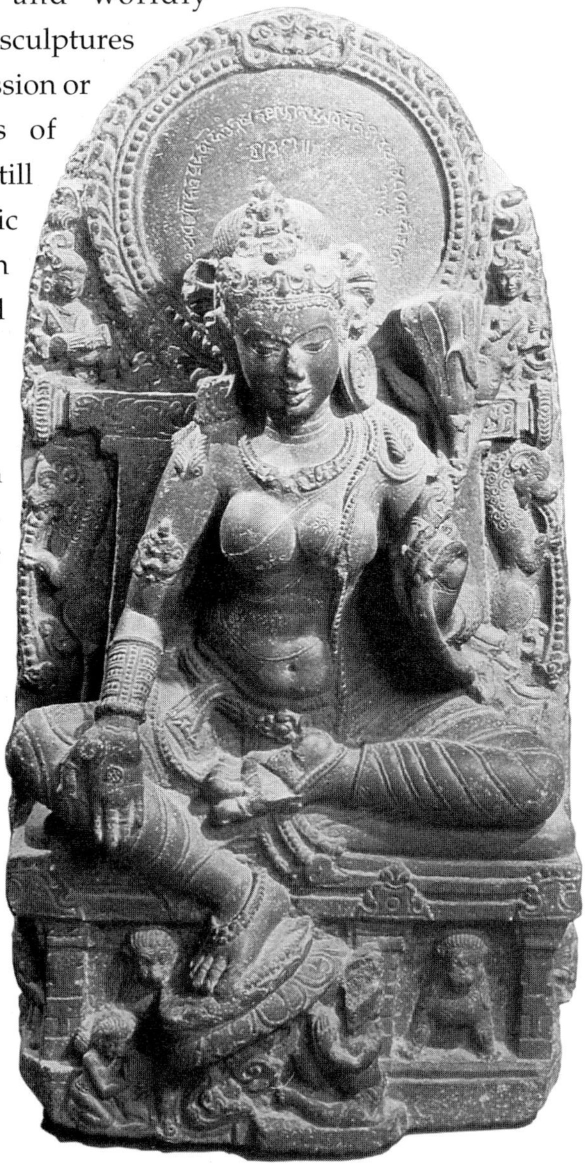

fig. 7. Tārā, Black stone, Tenth Century CE.

3. *Buddhacarita*, v.52.

4. How did dance come to stand for the symbolical articulation of life and the life process? Dance is flux, movement and any kind of movement can be perceived and measured in time alone, including the movement of the vital breath of life. When referred to in the abstract and in terms of eternity, it is Mahākāla; when measured in perceptual units of eternity, it is just Kāla, or change, and the unit of measurement is *tāla* or rhythmic beat as in dance. So the idea of dance as the symbol of articulation of life seems to lie therefore, in the traditional Indian concept of Time.

5. *Śiśupālavadha*, X.59, 60 & 65.

6. In the Khajurāho, in some of the panels the young girls were shown involved in the act of *śṛṅgāra* (decoration) of their bodies. One such female is shown as if she has just come out of bath and rinsing her hair. Another is seen engaged in looking in the mirror. Still another is seen going towards her lover. Then there are the trysting couples, involved in loving embrace. In other panel, the man bends down his head with the utmost tenderness over the face of the beloved, while she looks up with grace that could only permeate bodies imbued with the warmth of love.

7. The manifestation of a mental state through certain gestures is termed as *bhāva*. The classification of the types *nāyaka* and *nāyikā* was made in ancient literature according to their personality, nature, moods, character, physical features, age, experience and situation and then they further elaborated the classification according to their relationship such as — *nāyaka-anūkula* (sincere and devoted), *dakṣiṇa* (who love all women), *śaṭha* (unkind and false) and *dhṛṣṭa* (who does not care for wrong). The Sanskrit literature divided the *nāyikā*s according to there *jāti*, *guṇa* and appearance as follows — (1) *padminī* (lotus women), (2) *citriṇī* (graceful and full proportioned), (3) *śaṅkhinī* (conch-like) and (4) *hastinī* (heavy and coarse). Again according to their age and relationship they are further classified (a) *bālā* = 10 years to 14 years,

(b) *kanyā* = 14 years to 18 years, (c) *taruṇī* = 18 years to 30 years, (d) *prauḍhā* = 30 years to 55 years; as per relationship-*svakiyā* (one's own), *parakiyā* (another's), *sāmānyā* (anybody's). *Parakiyā* are further classified into *ūḍhā* (married) and *anūḍhā* (unmarried).

8. According to *Śabdakalpadruma*, the word of "beauty" is defined as a quality of that composite whole where balance, harmony and relation are uniformly maintained. The very unity in the diversity of the parts reflects the beauty of the forms.

9. All the arts were known to be interconnected by movement, so that we can see the figures in Indian art combine the body of a *yogī* and movement of a dancer; nature in her creative aspect was known as good dancer (breath was known as the principle of all living or moving form). This awareness was given permanent shape in art.

10. Ellorā has also other aspects of life to show, biological in meaning and significance, not only in the rock-cut temples but also in more than one other caves. These are all *mithuna* reliefs, in which figures are emerging out of the rock through themselves in violent embraces and rapturous kisses, life seeking to beget life by coming together and becoming one.

11. *R̥gveda*, IX.113.11.

12. It is true that in a few temples the sculptural art is found influenced by the Tantra, and the sensuous love of, and joy in, the human figures, may have been due to Tāntric inspiration; in all such images, the pliability and amplitude of the sensuous outline is the distinguishing feature which is responsible for the dynamic vitality, delightful abandon of feeling, emotion and action, an almost innocent but ecstatic joy of living, further characterized by a rich luxuriousness of appearance, and intense love for human body, as well as to communicate that this body is capable of yielding in terms of life-experience. But, is it a right interpretation and an explanation in the light of influence of Tantra? We know that

Tāntric *sādhanā* was not meant for pleasure but was undertaken as a ritual act and, in this light, only a few sculptures were found carved according to yogic discipline. The eternal bliss of the non-dual state is rarely reflected in the sculptural depictions. Only a handful sculptures of Orissa and Khajurāho present lovers in a state of bliss. The true Tāntric art is functionally related to the *upāsanā* and *sādhanā* to attain the non-dual *sahaja* state.

13. In *Saundaryalaharī*, written by Śaṅkarācārya in ninth century CE in praise of women, is present the redolence of love before he gave up the body as a "potful of dirt" —

    O Paragon of woman — thy waist was
    Too slender and curved even at thy birth,
    It's now a vanishing line what with thy
    Heavy breasts! It's now come to be fragile
    Like the tree on the bank of a gushing stream
    That has washed all earth from its roots away
    Kāma has wanton mady' thy golden breasts
    Hard so that thy might tear thy bodice, and
    Repose thy arm-pits, but, he could not harm
    Thy waist, for it's safe bound by three cardamom lines.

3

Masterpieces of Feminine Beauty

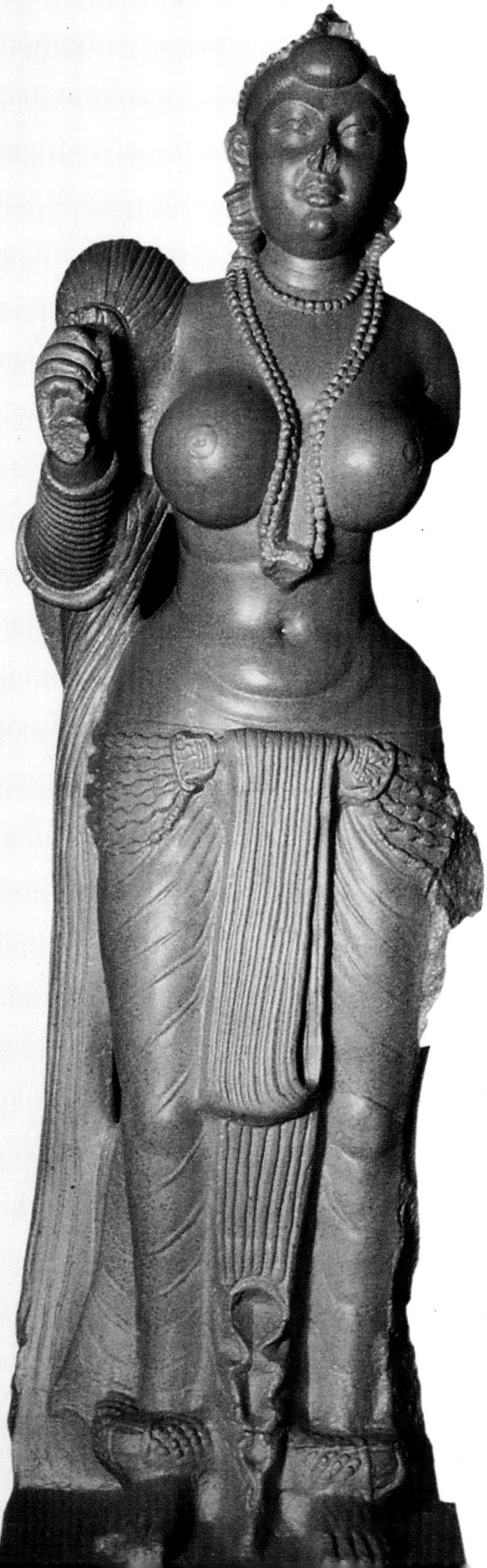

Plate 1. Yakṣī, Sandstone, Third Century BCE, Dīdārganj, Patna, Patna Museum

She appears as a unique example of feminine grace and beauty. According to *Śabdakalpadrum*, the term "beauty" denotes a quality of that composite whole the parts of which are held in proper balance, harmony and relation. Further it is added that it must have capacity to give pleasure to the perceiver. It thus recalls the description of a female beauty by Kālidāsa as under:

चित्रे निवेश्य परिकल्पित सत्वयोगा
    रुपोच्चयेनमनसा विधिना कृतानु ।
स्त्रीरत्नसृष्टिरपरा प्रतिभाति सा मे
    धातुर्विभुत्वभतुचिन्त्य वुपश्च तस्याः ॥

citre niveśya parikalpita satvayogā
    rūpoccayenamanasā vidhinā kṛtānu ।
strīratnasṛṣtiraparā pratibhāti sā me
    dhāturvibhutva bhatucintya vupaśca tasyāḥ ॥

— *Abhijñānaśākuntalam*, Dvitīyāṅka, 9

Was she delineated in a picture and then endowed with life? Or was she moulded in the creator's mind from a selection (assemblage) of lovely forms? When I meditate on the power of the creator, and on her lineaments, she appears to me like a match creation of the loveliest of women.

Plate 2. Yakṣī, Red Sandstone, Second Century CE, Mathurā

The young lady stands in graceful *tribhaṅga*. She holds the branch of an *aśoka* tree by her left hand while her right hand is in akimbo. The twist of her waist, the full and heavy pair of her breasts and her mysterious smile connect her with fertility cult. She is adequately sensuous and her appeal has been essentially provocative.

She reminds at the same time a line from *Vikramorvaśīyam* of Kālidāsa.

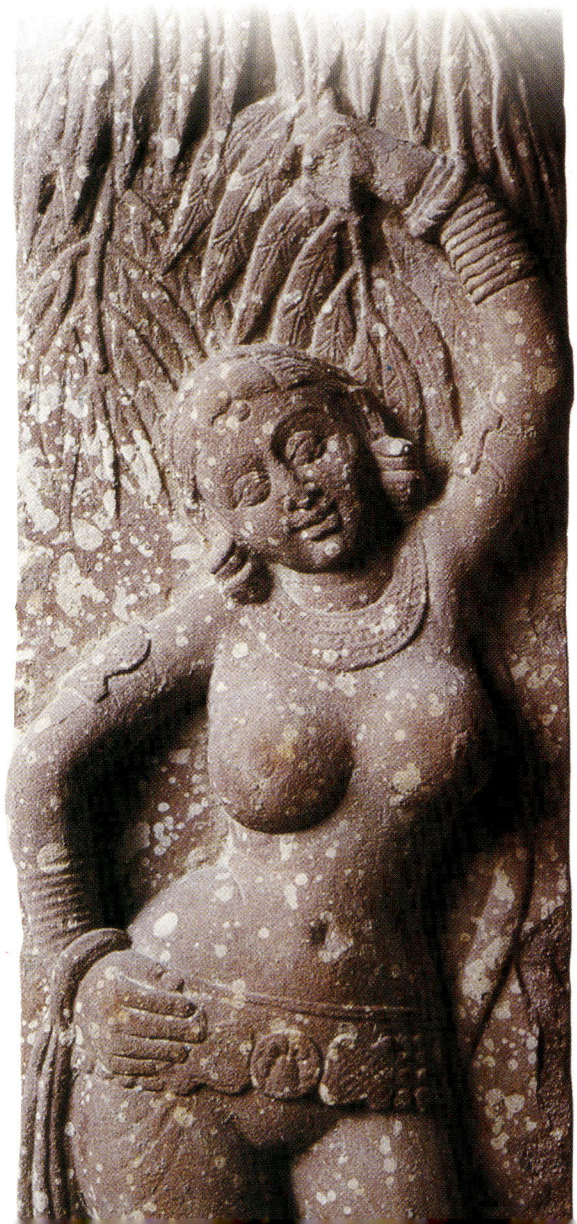

यदेवोपनतं दुःखात्सुखं तंद्रसक्त्तरम् ।
निर्वाणाय तरुच्छाया तप्तस्य हि विशेषतः ॥

yadevopanataṁ duḥkhātsukhaṁ
tandrasakttaram ।
nirvāṇāya tarucchāyā taptasya
hi viśeṣtaḥ ॥

— *Vikramorvaśīyam*, Dvitīyāṅka, 21

The joy that follows grief gains richer zest; the traveller who has been scorched by the fierce day can better tell how sweet is the shelter of the tree.

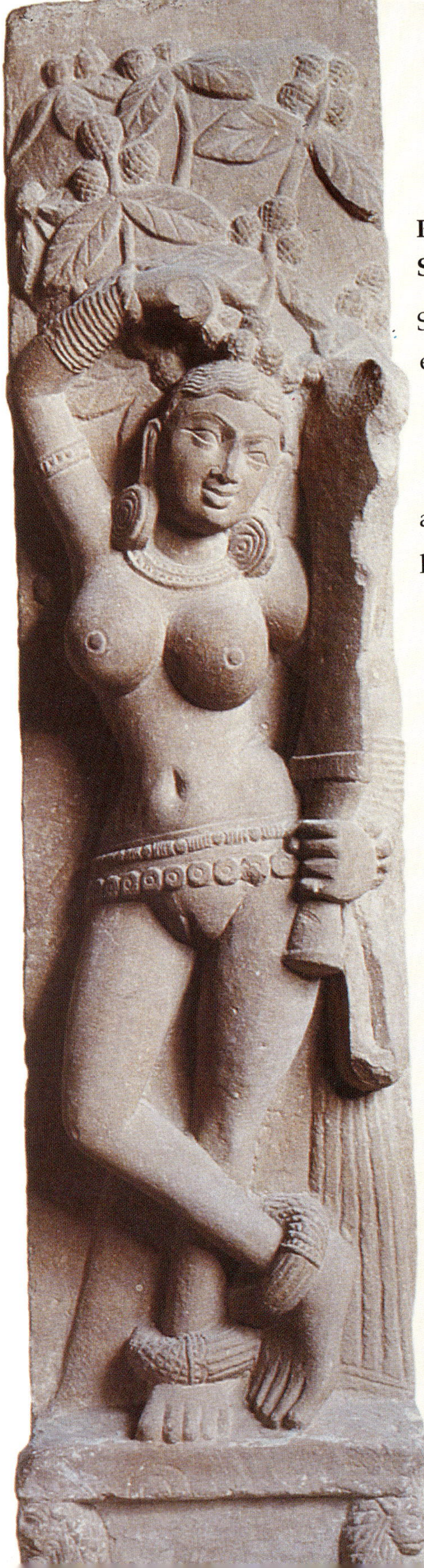

Plate 3. Attendant (Female figure), Red Sandstone, Second Century CE, Mathurā (U.P.)

She stands gracefully in *svastika* pose. She is endowed here with lush sensuality and careless abundance. With the raised right arm and slightly raised right bosom and with her coquettish countenance, this young female attendant appears like an enchantress, provocative and siren personified.

द्रुमा सुपुष्पा सलिलं सपद्मं
स्त्रियः सकामाः पवनः सुगन्धिः ।
सुखा प्रदोषा दिवसाश्च रम्याः
सर्वप्रिये चारुतरं बसन्ते ॥

drumā supuṣpā salilaṁ sapadmaṁ
striyaḥ sakāmāḥ pavanaḥ sugandhiḥ ।
sukhā pradoṣā divasāśca ramyāḥ
sarvapriye cārutaraṁ basante ॥

— *Ṛtusaṁhāra*, Ṣaṣthasarga, 2

My dear, Spring adorns whatever it touches — the trees put forth flowers; lotus in lakes; ladies are restless; the breeze is scented. Days and evenings are pleasant and delightful.

Plate 4. Woman and Scorpion, Red Sandstone, Fifth Century CE

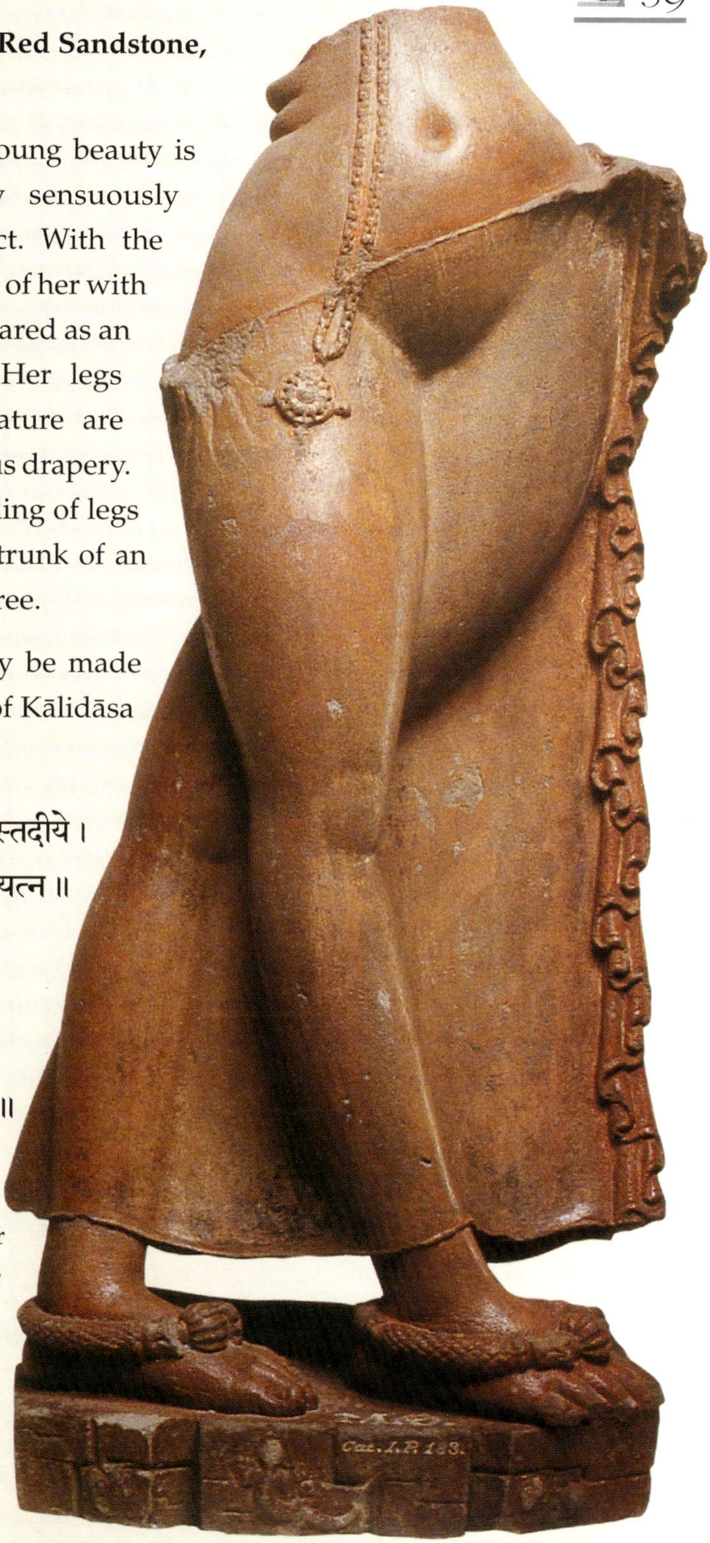

This surviving lower part of young beauty is enough to contemplate how sensuously charming she was when intact. With the partially exposed subdued belly of her with equally sensitive navel she appeared as an extremely passionate beauty. Her legs with smooth and resident feature are found covered with a diaphanous drapery. The plastic qualities and modelling of legs call for a comparison with the trunk of an elephant or of a young plantain tree.

Incidentally a reference may be made here from the *Kumārasaṁbhava* of Kālidāsa which runs thus:

वृत्तानुपूर्वे च न चातिदीर्घे जङ्घे सृष्टवतस्तदीये ।
शेषाङ्गनिर्माणाधौ विधातुर्लावण्य इवास यत्न ॥

vṛttānupūrve ca na cātidīrghe
jaṅghe sṛṣṭavatastadīye ।
śeṣāṅganirmārṇādhau
vidhāturlāvaṇya ivāsa yatna ॥

— *Sāhityadarpaṇa*, IV,
Prasannarāghava, I.37

The creator, having fashioned her legs, round and tapering from the knee down, had to make an effort in producing beauty for fashioning the remaining limbs.

or

> The trunks of elephants, because of the toughness of their skin and plantain-stalks, because of their extreme coolness, were outside the pale standards of comparison for her thighs.

Plate 5. Daughter of Māra? Cave I, Fifth Century CE, Ajantā

Before the attainment of enlightenment (*bodhi*) the conviction of the *bodhisattva* Gautama was challenged in a number of ways by the god Māra. The latter intended to disturb the concentration of the *bodhisattva* with the help of his beautiful daughters Rati, Rāga, and Tanhā. These daughters of Māra by the physical charms, sexual appeals of their lusty female forms and passionate movements tried their best to distract him but they utterly failed in their mission.

The unknown painters of Ajantā, in its classical phase tried to document this incident graphically in cave no. 1. The painting calls for a comparison with the description of a young *yakṣī* in the *Meghadūta* of poet Kālidāsa which runs thus:

> तन्वी श्यामा शिखरिदशना पक्वबिम्बाधरोष्ठी
> मध्ये क्षामा चकितहरिणीप्रेक्षणा निम्ननाभिः ।
> श्रोणी भारदलसगमना स्तोकनम्रा स्तनाभ्यां
> या यत्र स्याद्युवतिविषये सृष्टिराद्येव धातुः ॥

> *tanvī śyāmā śikharidaśanā pakvabimbādharoṣṭhī* ।
> *madhye kṣāmā cakitahariṇīprekṣaṇā nimnanābhiḥ* ॥
> *śroṇī bhārdalasagamanā stokanamrā stanābhyāṁ* ।
> *yā yatra syādyuvativiṣaye sṛṣṭirādyeva dhātuḥ* ॥

— *Meghadūta*, Uttermegh, 22

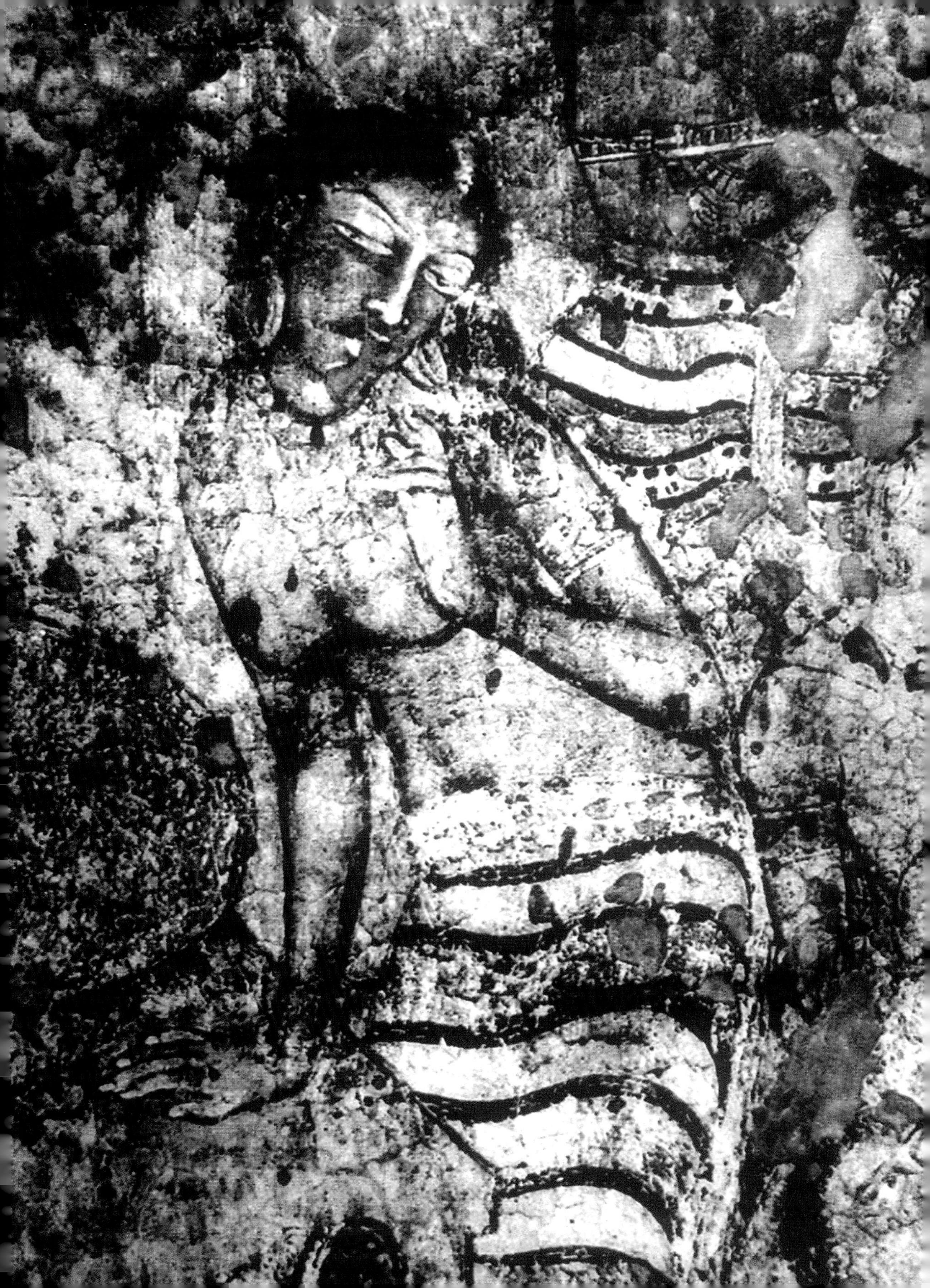

Slender and youthful, with even teeth, lip, red like *bimba* fruit, attenuated in waist, and glance like that of a startled deer; she has a deep navel, with a measured gait owing to the weight of the hips and she is slightly stooping from the weight of her bosom, she is as it were the first and the best in the creation of the feminine by the creator.

Succinctly put, probably there is no better example than the Temptation of Buddha by a daughter of Māra to illustrate effectively this description of Kālidāsa combining so many of the points of beauty in one. The side view of this is a graphic commentary on स्तोकनम्रा स्तनाभ्यां (slightly bent by her full breasts). The beauty of the attenuated waist and heavy hips as given in the line मध्ये क्षामा (attenuated in the waist) and श्रोणी भारदलसगमना (slow of gait or measured gait owing to the weight of the hips) are also clearly shown here. The eyes comparable to the frightened looks of the deer are indeed most charmingly formed as a part of a very graceful face. The navel in accordance with the canons of beauty in India is deep.

Plate 6. The Back View of a Young Lady, Cave XVII, Fifth Century CE, Ajantā

This gives the beautiful back view of a young seated lady. Seated leisurely, this personification of modesty is seen mildly adjusting her coiffure with her delicately drawn right hand while with the left hand she is seen balancing herself. Both covered and uncovered areas of her sensuous forms joined hands in exposing the aristocratic beauty in her. She reminds a couplet of *Meghadūta* which runs thus:

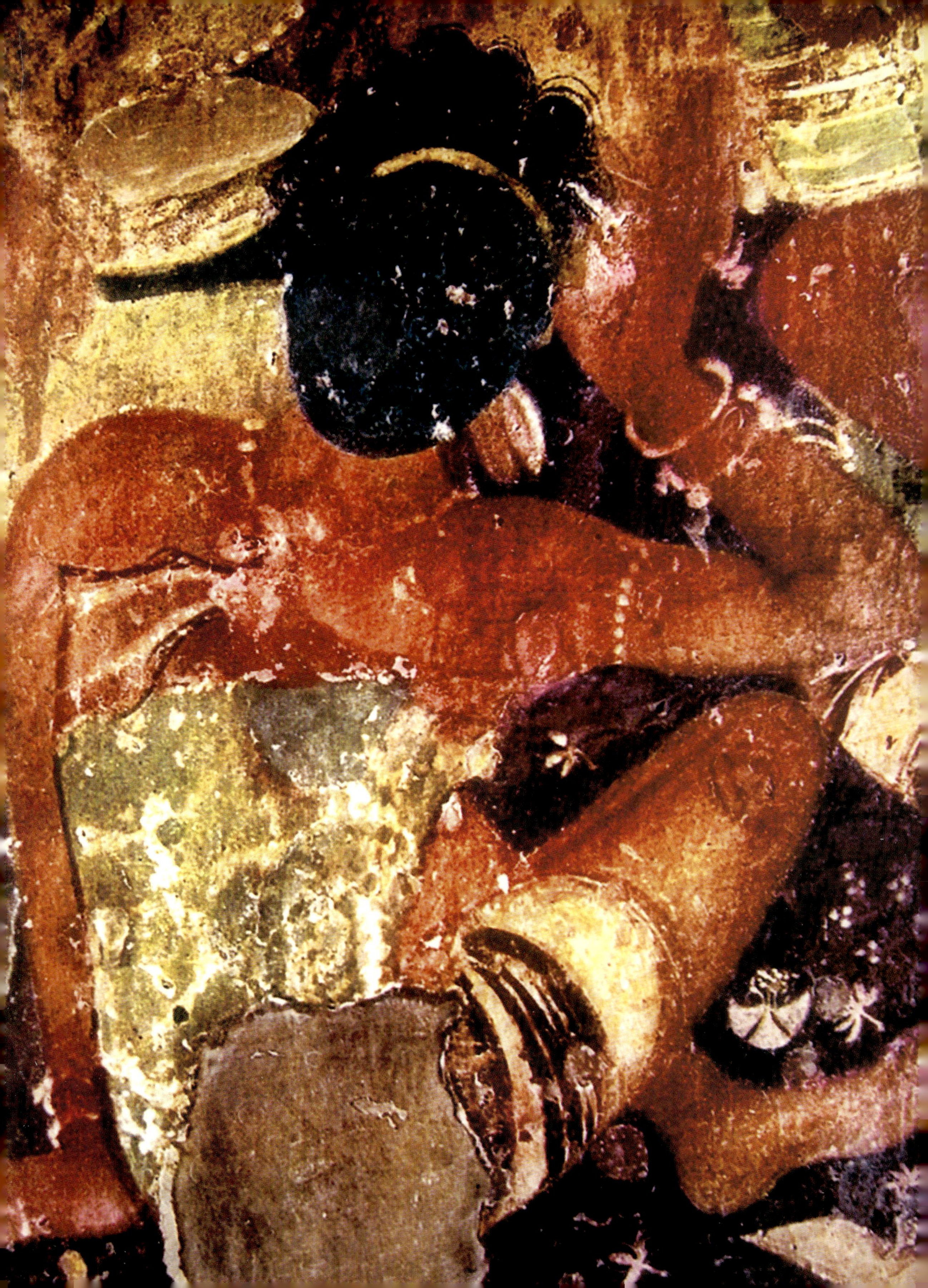

तस्या किंचित्कर घृतमिव प्राप्तवानीर शाखं,
हत्वा नीलं सलिलवसनं मुक्तरोधोनितम्बम ।
प्रस्थानं ते कथमपि सखे ! लम्बमानस्य भावि,
ज्ञातास्वादो विवृतजघनां को विहातुं समर्थः ॥

tasyā kiñcitkara ghṛtamiva prāptavānīra śākhaṁ,
hatvā nīlaṁ salilavasanaṁ muktarodhonitambam ॥
prasthānaṁ te kathamapi sakhe! lambamānasya bhāvi,
jñātāsvādo vivṛtajaghanāṁ ko vihātuṁ samarthaḥ ॥

— *Meghadūta* (Pūrvamegh), 45

Drawing away from her hips, the bank, her blue water-garment, which seems half-heartedly held by her hand, as reed branches hand touch it; bending over her, my friend! it will be hard for thee to depart, who, that has known love's savour (taste) can leave one whose haunches are bared (uncovered)?

Plate 7. Nokhas, Stone, Tenth Century CE, Bengal

दीर्घाक्षं शरदिन्दुकान्ति वदनं बाहू नतावंसयोः ।
संक्षिप्तं निविडोन्नतस्तनमुरः पार्श्वे प्रमृष्टे इव ॥
मध्यः पाणिमितो नितम्बि जघनं पादावरालङ्गुली ।
छन्दो नर्तयितुर्यथैव मनसिश्लिष्टं तथास्या वपुः ॥

dīrghākṣaṁ śaradindukānti vadanaṁ bāhū natāvaṁsayoḥ ।
saṁkṣiptaṁ niviḍonnatastanamuraḥ pārśve pramṛṣṭe iva ॥
madhyaḥ pāṇimito nitambi jaghanaṁ pādāvarālaṅgulī ।
chando nartayituryathaiva manasiśilaṣṭaṁ tathāsyā vapuḥ ॥

— *Mālavikāgnimitram*, Dvitīyāṅka, 2-3

When I behold her picture, I thought she should believe the loveliness of it; but now I think the artist who painted her likeness had not secured full concentration.

> How flawless in every part is her form —
>
> Her long eyes, her face lovely like the moon of autumn, the arm sloping at the shoulders; her compact bosom with the plump and swelling breasts, her side as if polished; her waist measurable by this palm of the hand; her hips expansive, her feet with the curved toes, her whole body thus seems framed to suit the fancy of her teacher of dancing.

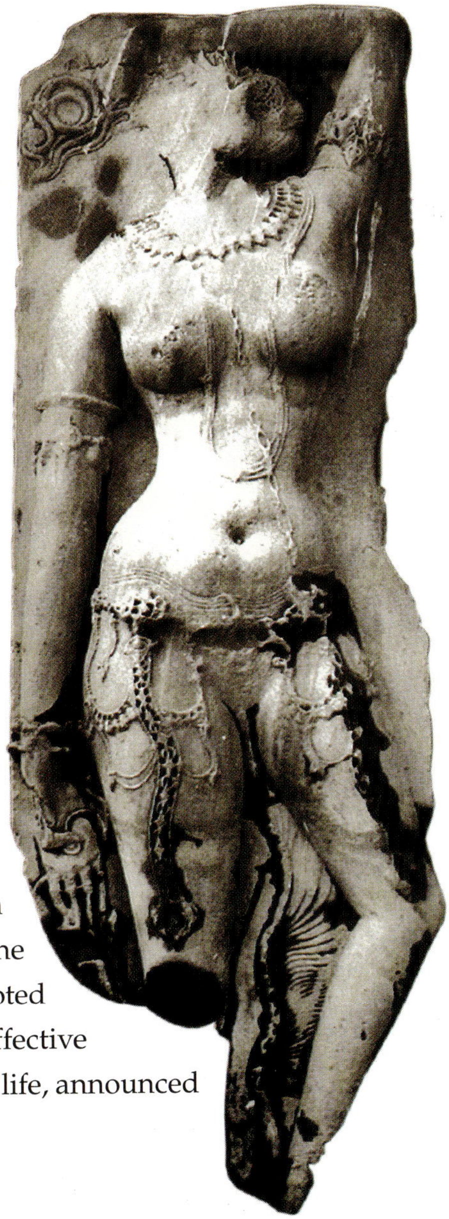

The joyous and effortless existence of life is here taken for granted. Everything here is thin, light and obvious, and frankly there is no trace of spiritual quest. The figure just bursts forth like flowers into light from the body. The unbounded love, joys of life both sensual and worldly, are clearly found laid bare in this tall and graceful figure of this enticing female.

The main impact, however, is made not by proportions of figure, but by the subtle and detailed interpretation of feminine beauty and that too on its animate surface. The artist's chisel glided caressingly along this living organism; everywhere halting to record the infinitesimal form of some subtle nuance. The relief, indeed, is not based on sensations of the eye, though the eye is invited to enjoy it. Such an intimate knowledge of the female body could not have been derived mainly from the observation of a standing female or from a recollection of primarily visual impressions. It is the product and expression of the sense of touch of devoted familiarity and experience in love, from which an effective intuition has been derived of the secret of the inner life, announced in the beauty of the forms.

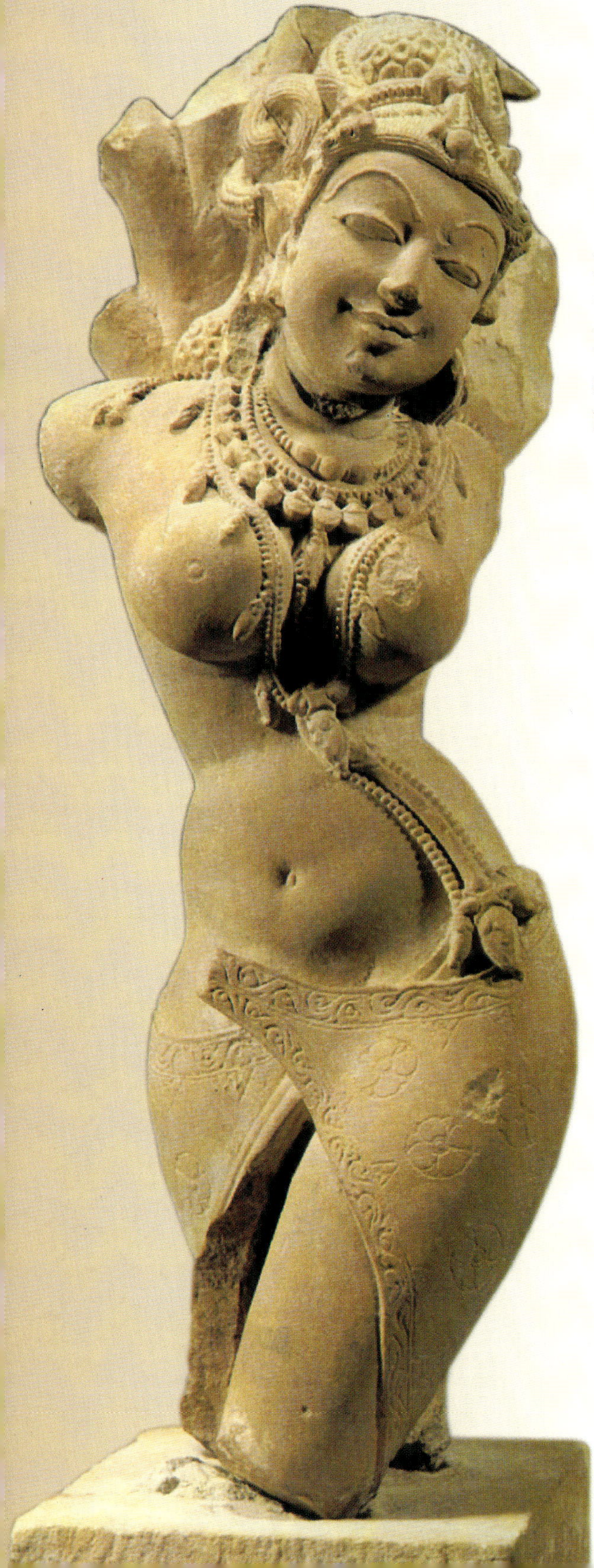

Plate 8. A Yakṣī, Sandstone, Eleventh Century CE

This mutilated young figure represents perhaps a personified modesty. Very delicately attained and bejewelled, the happy and smiling young lady exhibits a soft sensualism in her form. This mute beauty wants to speak that:

> "So long as lips shall kiss,
> and eyes shall see
> so long lives this,
> and this gives life to thee."

Plate 9. Lady in Languor (Alasākanyā), Sandstone, Eleventh Century CE, Khajurāho

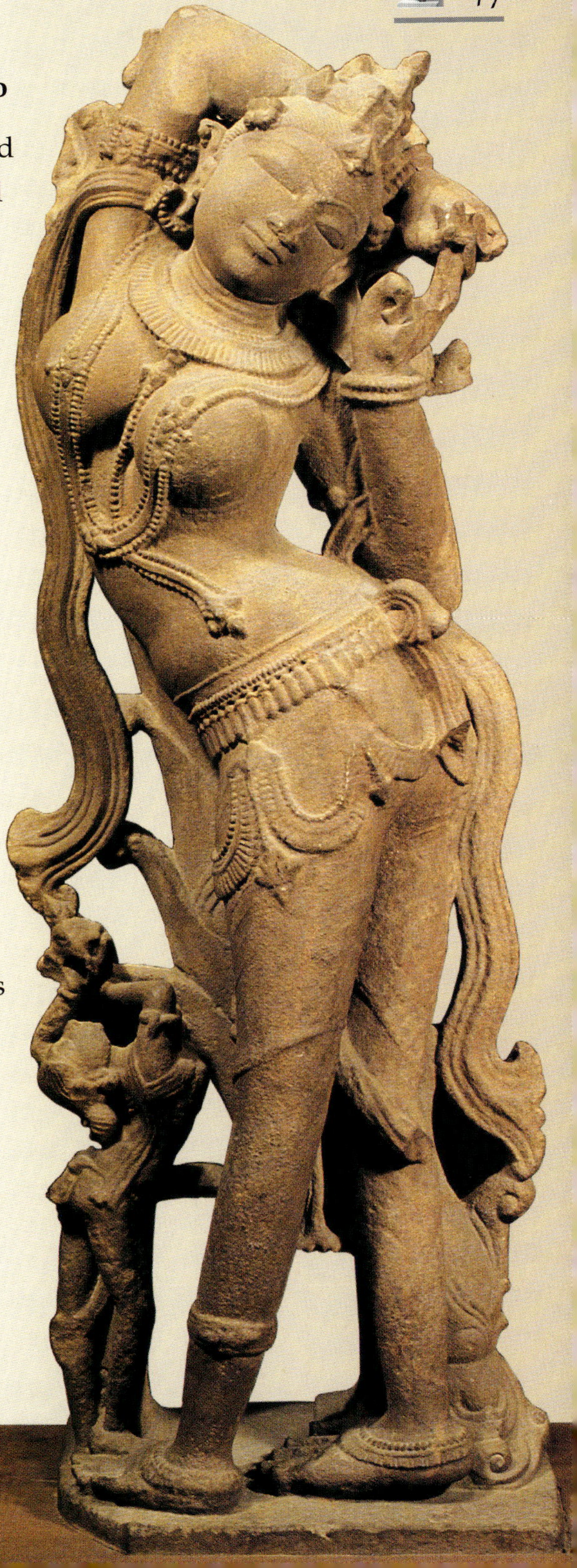

This young lady appears to have just awakened from her deep slumber and is yawning and that moment has been stilled here. This shows in the search for the most beautiful form the artist freezed this moment. The figure also reminds us two lines from *Ṛtusaṁhāra* of Kālidāsa which run thus:

तनूनि पाण्डूनि मदालसानि
मुहुर्मुहुर्जृम्भणतत्पराणि ।
अङ्गान्यनङ्ग प्रमदाजनस्य करोति
लावण्यससंभ्रमाणि ॥

tanūni pāṇḍūni madālasāni
muhurmuhurjṛmbhaṇa-tatparāṇi ।
aṅgānyanaṅga pramadājanasya
karoti lāvaṇyasa-saṁbhramāṇi ॥

The *Ṛtusaṁhāra* (cycle of seasons), of Kālidāsa describes spring season and its related sensation—

> The bodyless god of love make the body of women thin, pale, languid, waning at intervals, flurried with beauty; love is manifest all over the body; restless in eyes, languid with wine, pale in cheek, deep in waist, plump in their hips.

Plate 10. Pārvatī, Sandstone, Eleventh Century CE, Varanasi

The mutilated figure of Pārvatī is depicted in this as being four-handed and is standing erect (*samapāda-sthānaka*) presumably in a meditative pose (*tapasvinī*). Characterized by certain medieval traits of Indian art, this young figure recalls a few lines from *Saundaryalaharī* which runs thus:

स्थिरो गङ्गावर्तः स्तनमुकुलरोमावलिलता। निजावहं कुण्डं कुसुमशरतेजोहुतभुजः॥
निसर्गक्षीणस्य स्तनतटभरेण क्लमजुषो। नमन्मूर्तेर्नारीतिलक शनकैस्त्रुटयत इव॥
कुचौ सद्यःस्विद्यत तटघटित कूर्पासभिदुरौ। क्षन्तौ दोर्मूले कनककलशाभो कलयता॥

sthiro gaṅgāvartaḥ stana-mukula-romāvalilatā ।
nijāvahaṁ kuṇḍaṁ kusumaśara-tejo-hutabhujaḥ ॥
nisarga-kṣīṇasya stana-taṭa-bhareṇa klamajuṣo ।
namanmūrter-nārītilak śanakais-truṭayata iva ॥
kucau sadyaḥ-svidyat taṭa-ghaṭita kūrpāsa-bhidurau ।
kṣantau dormūle kanaka-kalaśābhau kalayatā ॥

This (80) stanza gives a description of the navel as assuming various aspects of Kusumāśara — literally the flower arrowed, i.e. Manmatha, the god of love. The Devīs navel is compared to such a spot resting in which the eyes of Girīśa (as so many *yogins*) seek to attain bliss.

O Daughter of the Mountain! may safety be vouchsafed to thy waist, which by nature is slim and which is in the form as if about to give way in the region of the navel and the fold, and whose firmness is akin to that of a tree standing on the fragile bank of a river. (79)

Thy threefolded waist has been found as it were by Tanubhū (Manmatha, the god of love), three times over with the *lavale* creeper, with a view to save it from breaking; he having caused thy two breasts, which resemble pots of gold, to burst the garment covering their sides perspiring at that moment and to rub against the armpits. Her breasts were not sucked so far and therefore they look full and firm (*apītakucā*).

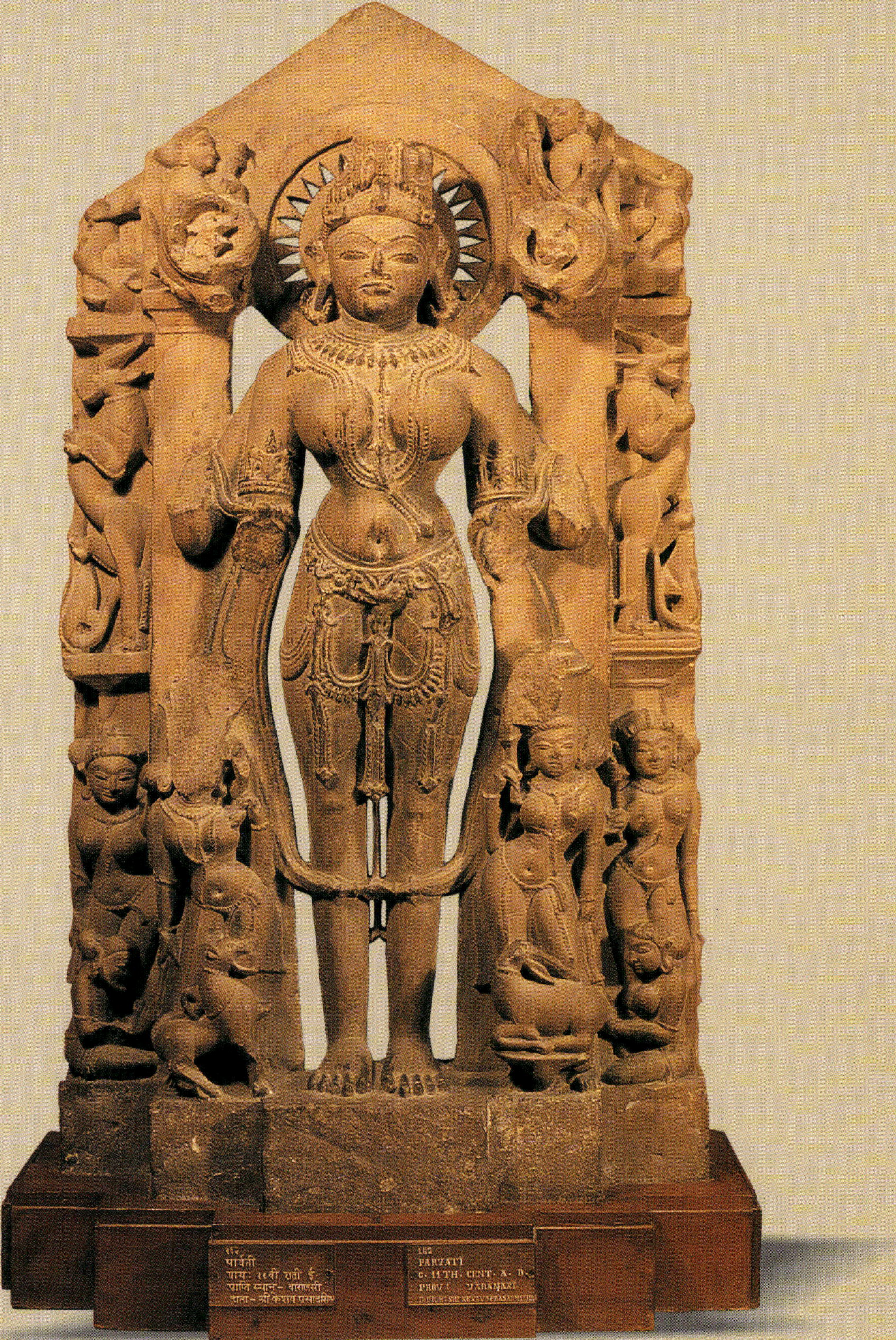
पार्वती
162
PARVATI
C. 11 TH. CENT. A. D.
PROV: VARANASI

Plate 11. Mithuna, Sandstone, Eleventh Century CE

The panel exposes an intimate sexual scene — it shows the preparatory stage of a sexual game. The manipulation of the two hands of the lover has been very deftly and skilfully realized and the sculptor knew where he had to stop. The partial exposure of the sex organ and the mild pressure on the left breast of the female participant are enough to excite the participants as well as its viewers.

The beautiful verse of Māgha — where the tender approach in love contrasted with rude coarse intrusion is clearly set forth. The half-closed eyes of the damsel suggesting the great pleasure and satisfaction with which she beams and of which her face is a great index, like that of her lover, described in a verse.

When the hand of the lovers crossed the waist-knot, she with her eyes half-closed sweetly ejaculated with lips as if it were the sweet twang of the strings of a lute struck by a passionate lyrist (*Śiśupālavadha*, X.64). Again this sculpture reminds us of the verse in *Meghadūta*, where, when lover's hand is on the knot of the garment to free it, the lady, being shy, tries in vain to put it out.

Another exquisite sculpture from Bhuvaneshwar presents the sporting of the lover's hand on the body of the beloved one as described in the verse of the *Mahābhārata* —

अयं स रशनोत्कर्षी पीनस्तन विमर्दनः ।
नाभ्यूरुजघनस्पर्शी नीवीविस्त्रसन करः ॥

ayaṁ sa raśanotkarṣī pīnastana vimardanaḥ ।
nābhyūrujghanasparśī nīvīvistrasana karaḥ ॥

— *Mahābhārata*, XI.24, 19

This type of *nāyikā* is known as *ākrānta-nāyikā*, after her sport with *nāyaka* and again on his touch experiencing horripilation and almost unconscious with a reeling sensation of joy born of passion.

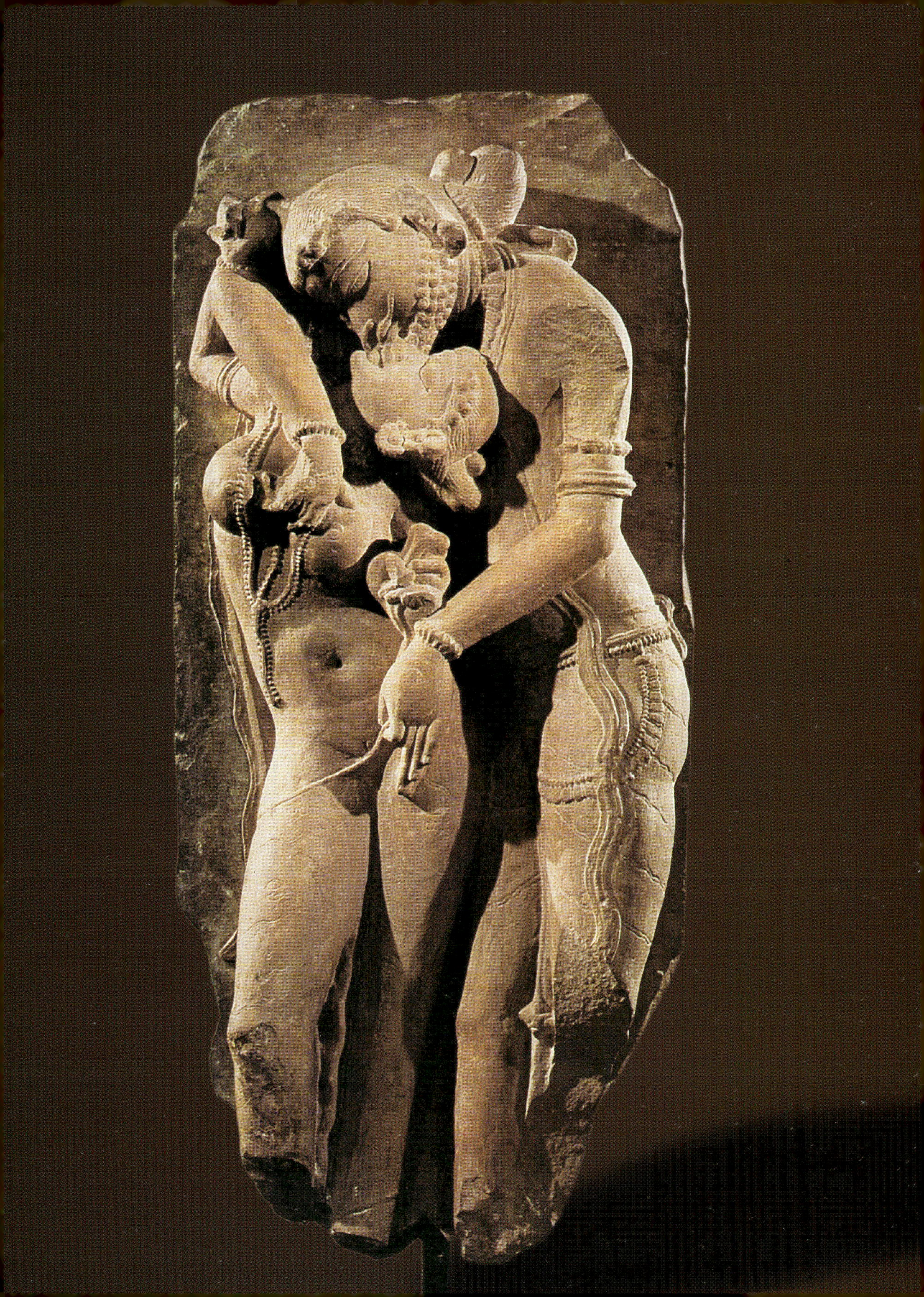

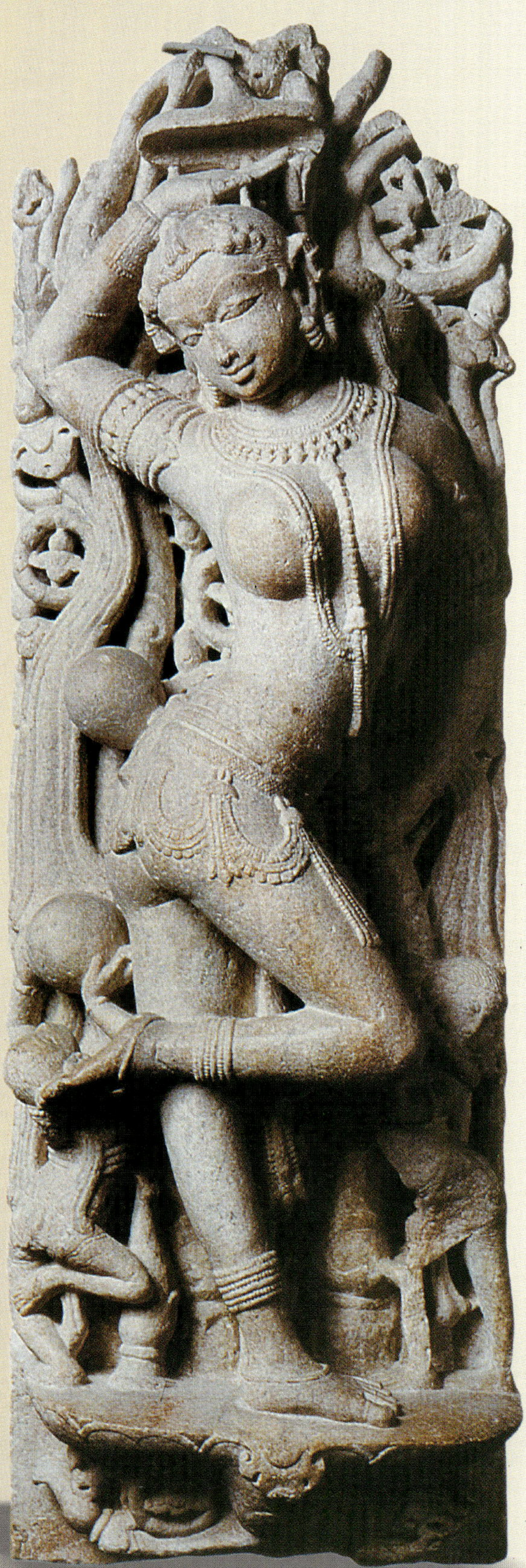

Plate 12. The Maiden, Eleventh Century CE, National Museum, New Delhi

While searching the exact posture and the right moment when a young damsel looks most beautiful, the sculptor went for this image. The young beauty gracefully turns back to see the sole of her right foot raised if it was struck by a stone chip or a thorn! Her sensuous form becomes exposed maximum at this stage and therefore, it was stilled for ever.

If the verse in Kālidāsa's *Abhijñāna-śākuntalam*, describing a beautiful pose of Śakuntalā with her face turned back for a last look at Duṣyanta before parting with one of her feet raised on the pretext of removing a thorn is a masterpiece of literary picture. There are numerous such in sculpture, for *bhaṅga*s or flexions enhance the natural beauty of form by appropriate rhythmic curves and movements of the body.

13. Mohinī (temptress), Sandstone, Eleventh Century CE

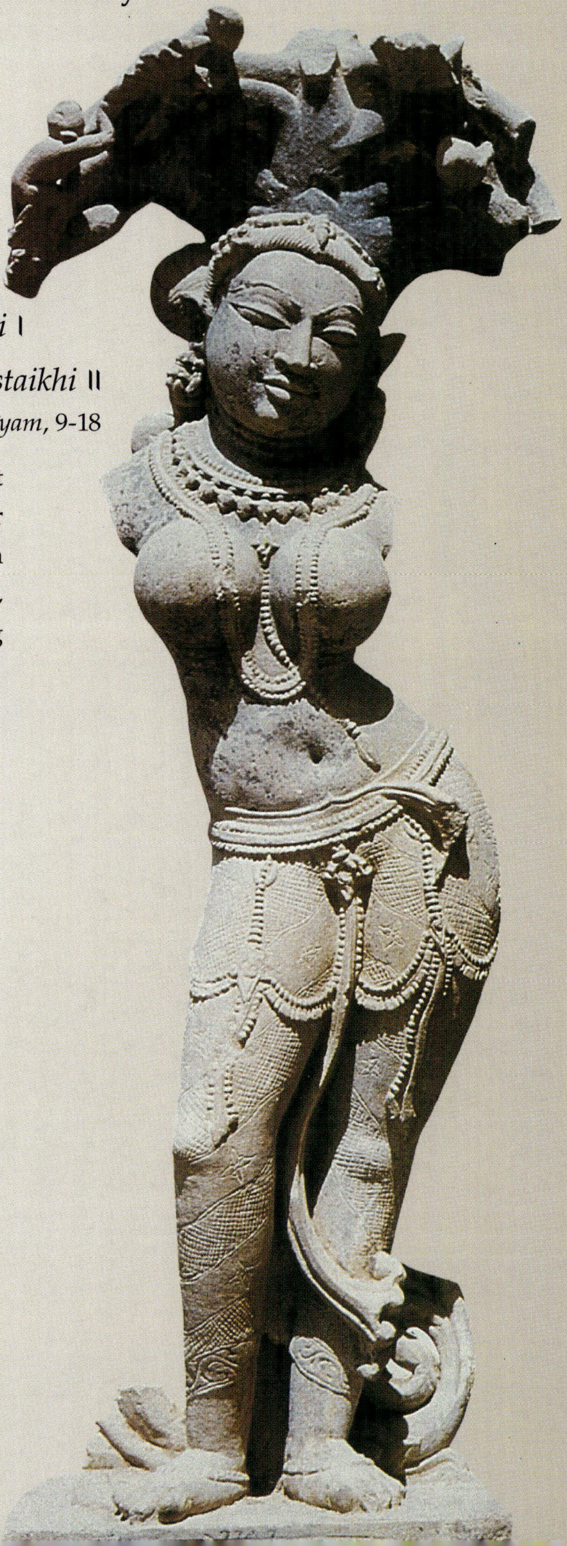

अनीशया शरीरस्य स्ववशं हृदयं मयि ।
स्तनकम्पक्रियालक्ष्यैर्न्यस्तं निःश्वासतैखि ॥

anīśayā śarīrasya svavaśaṁ hr̥dayaṁ mayi ।
stanakampakriyālakṣyairnyastaṁ niḥśvāstaikhi ॥

— *Vikramorvaśīyam*, 9-18

My mind is filled with the same hope. For at the time of departing, she not mistress of her own person, seemed to lodge her heart in mine, free as she was to dispose of it, through her sighs indicated by the panting of the bosom.

Plate 14. Surasundarī, Sandstone, Eleventh Century CE

She has been identified as the mutilated figure of celestial beauty (*Surasundarī*), while her face retains certain divine qualities her mutilated torso is found endowed with qualities of earthly beauty. Her massive shoulder, a pair of heavy breasts and attenuated waist call for a comparison with *mānavī*.

The great love with which the wine cup is offered to the beloved or received from her is beautifully expressed by Kālidāsa in this line:

मुखार्पणेषु प्रकृतिप्रगल्भाः स्वयं तरङ्गाधरदानदक्षः ।
अनन्यसामान्यकलत्रवृत्तिः पिबत्यसौ पाययते च सिंधू ॥

mukhārpaṇeṣu prakṛtipragalbhāḥ svayaṁ taraṅgādhara-dānadakṣaḥ ।
ananyasāmānyakalatravṛttiḥ pibatyasau pāyayate ca sindhū ॥

— *Raghuvaṁśa*, XIII.9

> This (ocean) with a rare quality of spouse, not found in other; himself drinks and causes to drink the rivers that are bold in offering their mouth, himself and adept in offering his wavy lips.

And by the Māgha in the *Śiśupālavadha*, X.23:

दतमादत्तभदनं दयितेन ब्याप्तमातिशयिकेन रसेन ।
सस्वदे मुखसुरं प्रमदाभ्यो नाम रुढमपि च व्युद्रपादि ॥

datamādattabhadanaṁ dayitena byāptamātiśayikena rasena ।
sasvade mukhasuraṁ pramadābhyo nāma ruḍhamapi ca vyudrapādi ॥

> Passionately given by the beloved one and hence all the more suffused with taste the mouthfuls of wine were enjoyable to the damsels.

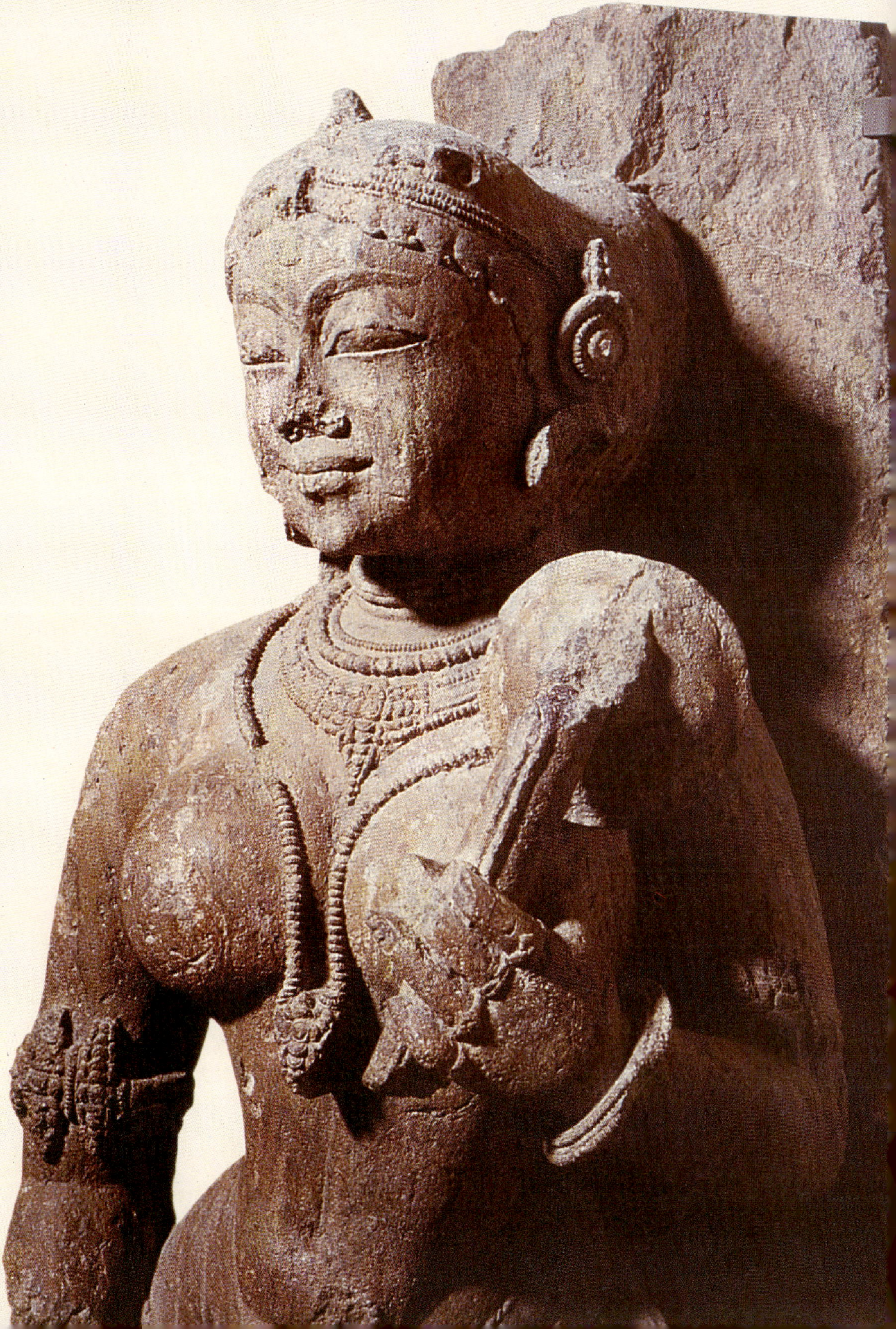

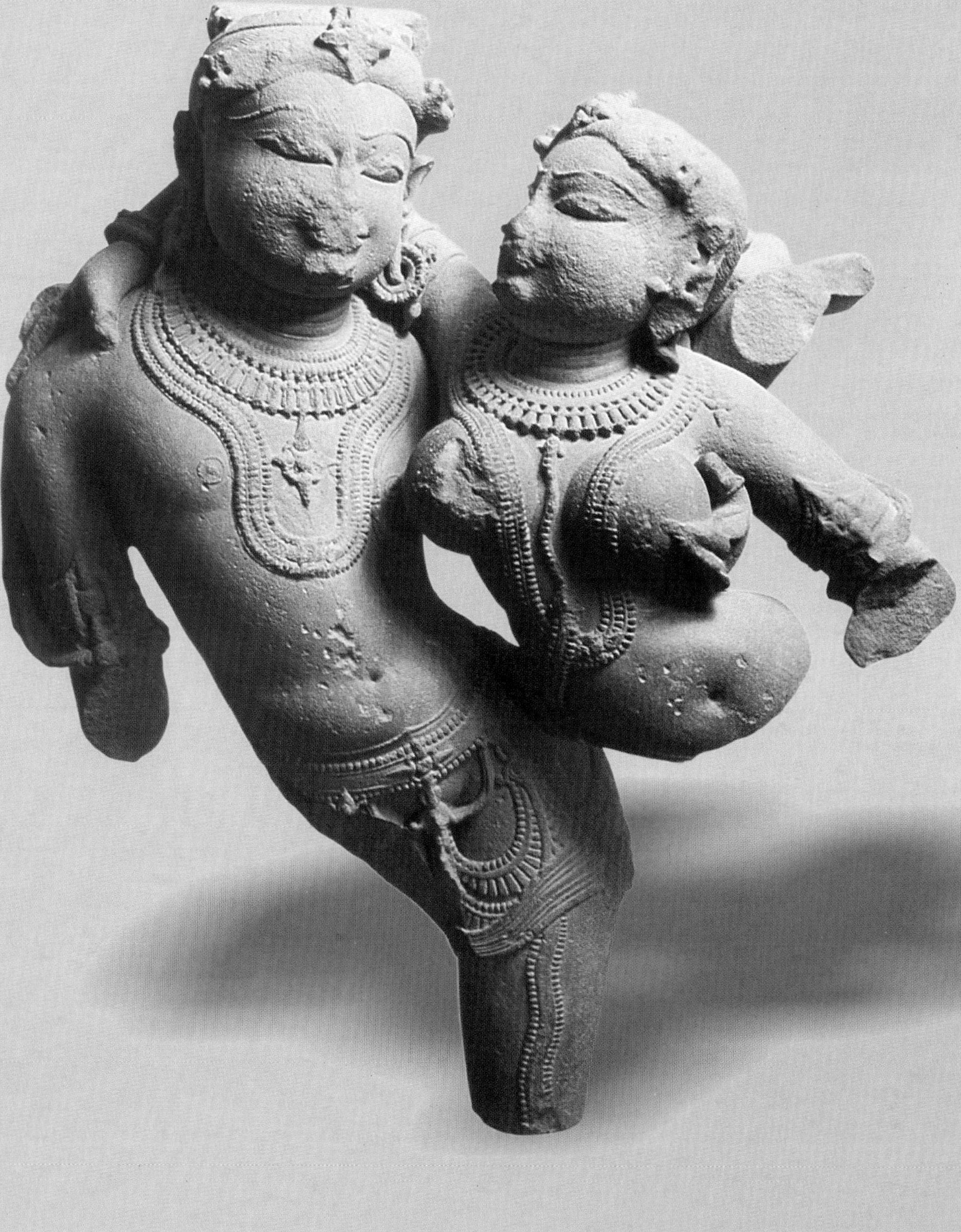

Plate 15. Couple of Embrace, Sandstone, Eleventh Century CE

This depicts a mutilated figure of an amorous couple. The heroine here appears more passionate. Her passion has been charged by her partner who with his left hand is seen mildly stroking the left bosom of his spouse. On her softly modelled belly, the incorporation of deep navel enhanced her passionate feelings more. The male counterpart seemingly looks happy but he appears to be a matured actor in this love game:

> अङ्गानि निद्रालसविभ्रमाणि वाक्यानि किञ्चिन्मदिरालसानि ।
> भ्रूक्षेपजिह्वानि च वीक्षितानी चकार काम प्रमदाजनानाम ॥
>
> *aṅgāni nidrālasavibhramāṇi*
> *vākyāni kiñcinmadirālasāni* ।
> *bhrūkṣepajihvāni ca vīkṣitānī*
> *cakāra kāma pramadājanānāma* ॥
>
> — *Ṛtusaṁhāra*, 6.13
>
> Love makes a special gift to women: limbs, a little sleepy and lazy; speech, a little slurred with wine and glances crossed by the elevation of eyebrows.

Ordinarily it may mean nothing more than an amorous couple, it has given us loveliest commentaries.

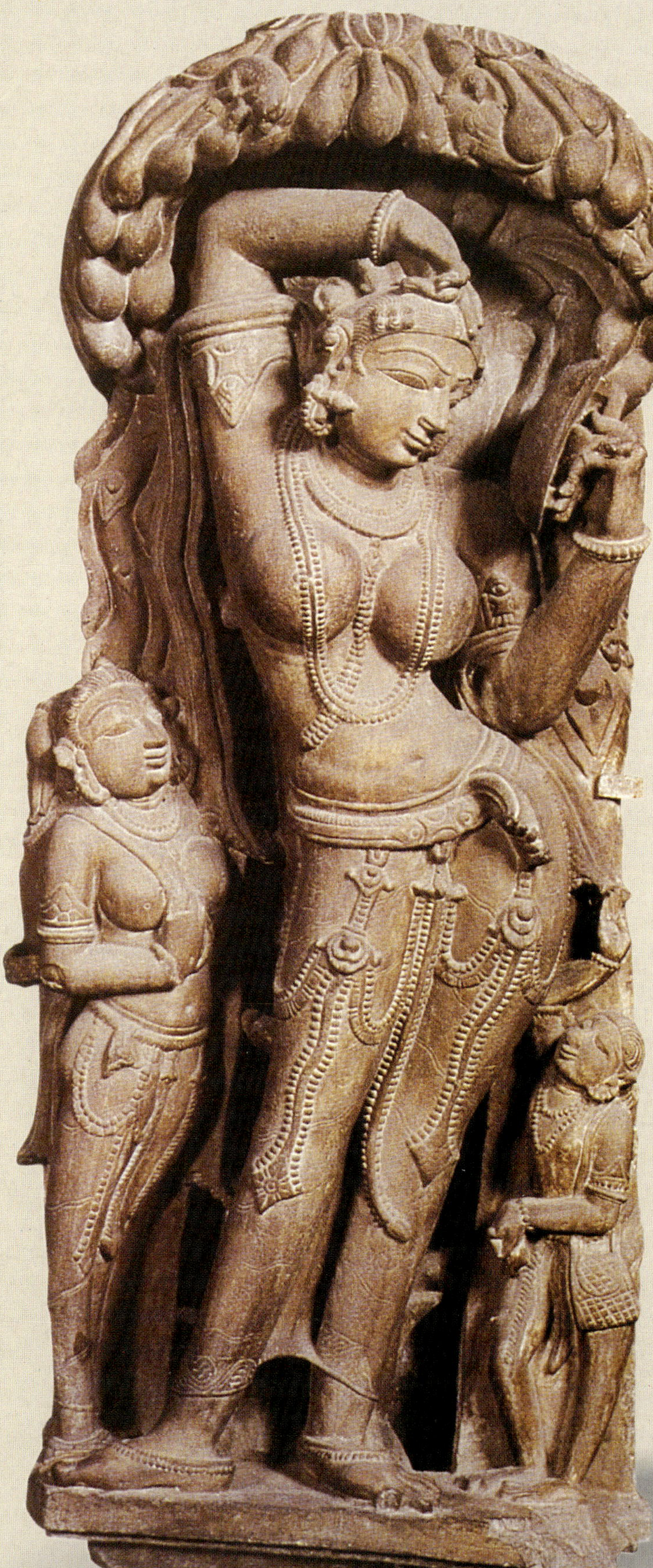

16. Lady with Mirror, Sandstone, Eleventh Century CE

This young beauty is shown here engaged in her toilets. She is conscious of her beauty and adequately concerned to maintain it. Her graceful standing posture and her young form have adequate sensitivity and charming qualities.

अथ मधुवनितानां नेत्रनिर्वेशनीयं
मनसिजतरुपुष्पं रागबन्धप्रवालम् ।
अकृतकविधि सर्वाङ्गीणमाकल्पजातं
विलसितपदमाद्यमं यौवनं सः प्रपेदे ॥

atha madhuvanitānāṁ netranirveśanīyaṁ
manasijatarupuṣpaṁ rāgabandhapravālam ।
akr̥takavidhi sarvāṅgīṇamākalpajātaṁ
vilsitapadamādyamaṁ yauvanaṁ saḥ prapede ॥

— *Raghuvaṁśa*, 18 *Sarga*, 52

She attained youthful age, prime home of grace, wine to be relished by the eyes of young damsels, flower of the tree of love, with passion for young shoots, natural ornaments, embellishing the entire body.

Plate 17. Gaṅgā, Black Stone, Twelfth Century CE, Bengal

This profusely jewelled torso of female was carved in black chlorite and may be stylistically dated to twelfth century CE. This was a phase of Indian sculpture which may be described in Western form — a period of baroque or rococo. The face of this thick-set young female is found pervaded with a sad and gloomy look. It appears that she is suffering from the pangs of separation of his lord and she has turned as the personification of melancholy.

There is hardly any human being who can remain unaffected with the change in conditions. The following lines provide striking example of a state of mind during separation:

> बिरह-अवधि अवगाह अपारा, कोटि मंच इक परिय ते पारा ।
> बिरह कि जगत अबिरथा जाहि, बिरह रूप यह शृष्टि सबाहि ॥
>
> *biraha-avadhi avagāha apārā, koṭi mañca ika pariya te pārā* ।
> *biraha ki jagata abirathā jāhi, biraha rūpa yaha śṛṣṭi sabāhi* ॥
>
> — *Madhumālatī*, Kavimajjhan

> The above lines give a gist of Sufi philosophy. The poet says that if one is suffering from separation (obviously from the company of God and heaven) one's heart becomes sensitive like a mirror in which many reflections can be seen. He finds that her (*Madhumālatī*) whole world is manifestation of his own sufferings.

The expression retains a certain ambivalence; it has more charm than mystery. The face of the image registers the reflex of psychological expression and her eyes betray as if they are absorbed within themselves.

In this image of Gaṅgā the new quality can be felt. The figure was completely conceived in lower Ganges conception embodying sentiment and a revelation of vitality and sweetness, youth and beauty, such as the artist beheld her everyday. The goddess apparently personifies a vision of health and wealth, prosperity and abundance, dignity and prowess. She represents joy in this life on earth and also hope for the life to come, hence she is styled "The Mother who both bestows happiness and prosperity (*sukhadā*) and secure salvation hereafter (*mokṣadā*)." The epitome of feminine beauty, stands in graceful solemnity and benign repose, clad in her festive attire and rich jewels perhaps to procreate new life. Art has been clarified and resynthesized in term of a new ideal. A meaningful balance and perfect harmony have been attained between the earthly material from which the image has been made and the concept that it symbolizes.

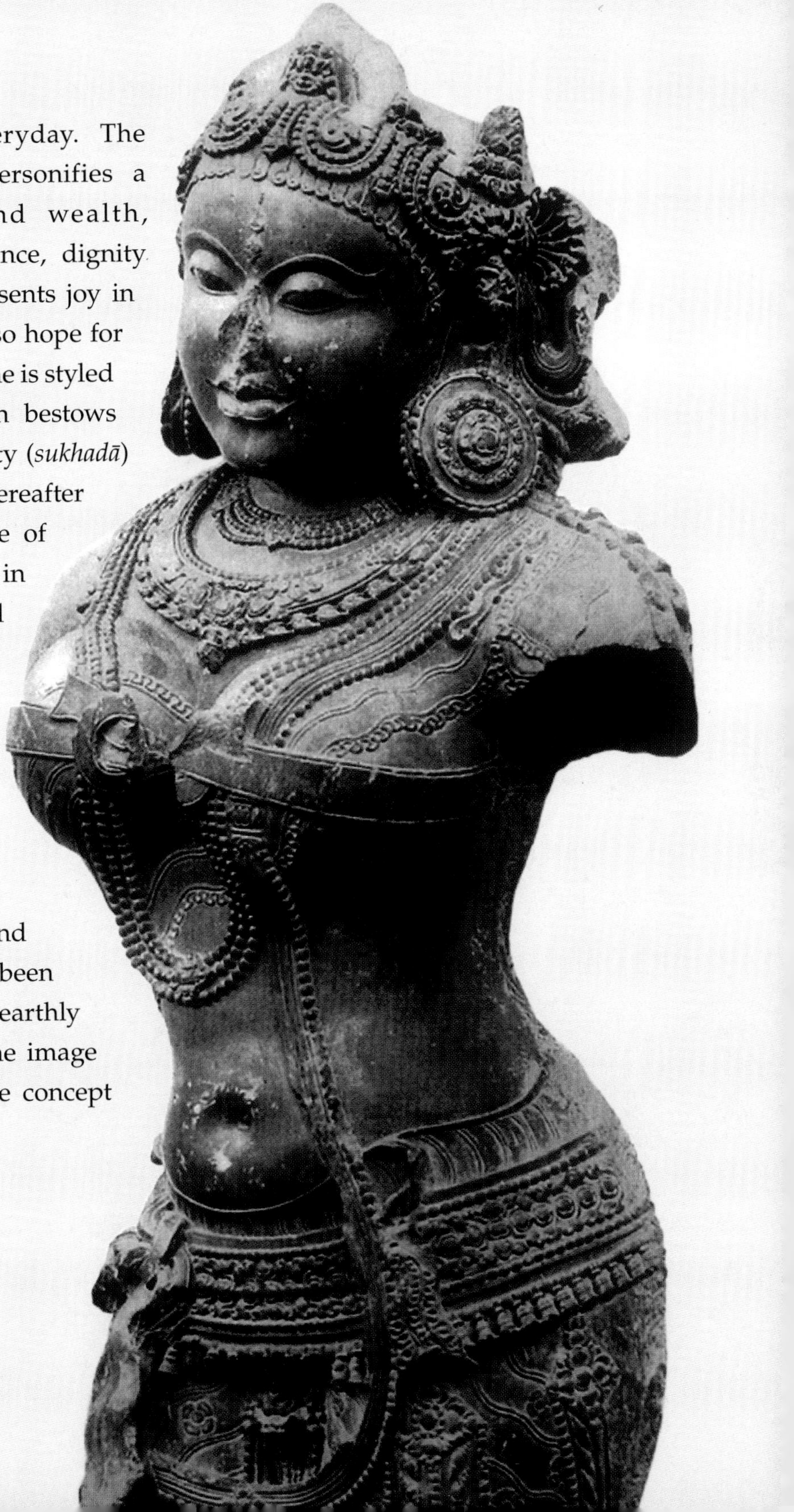

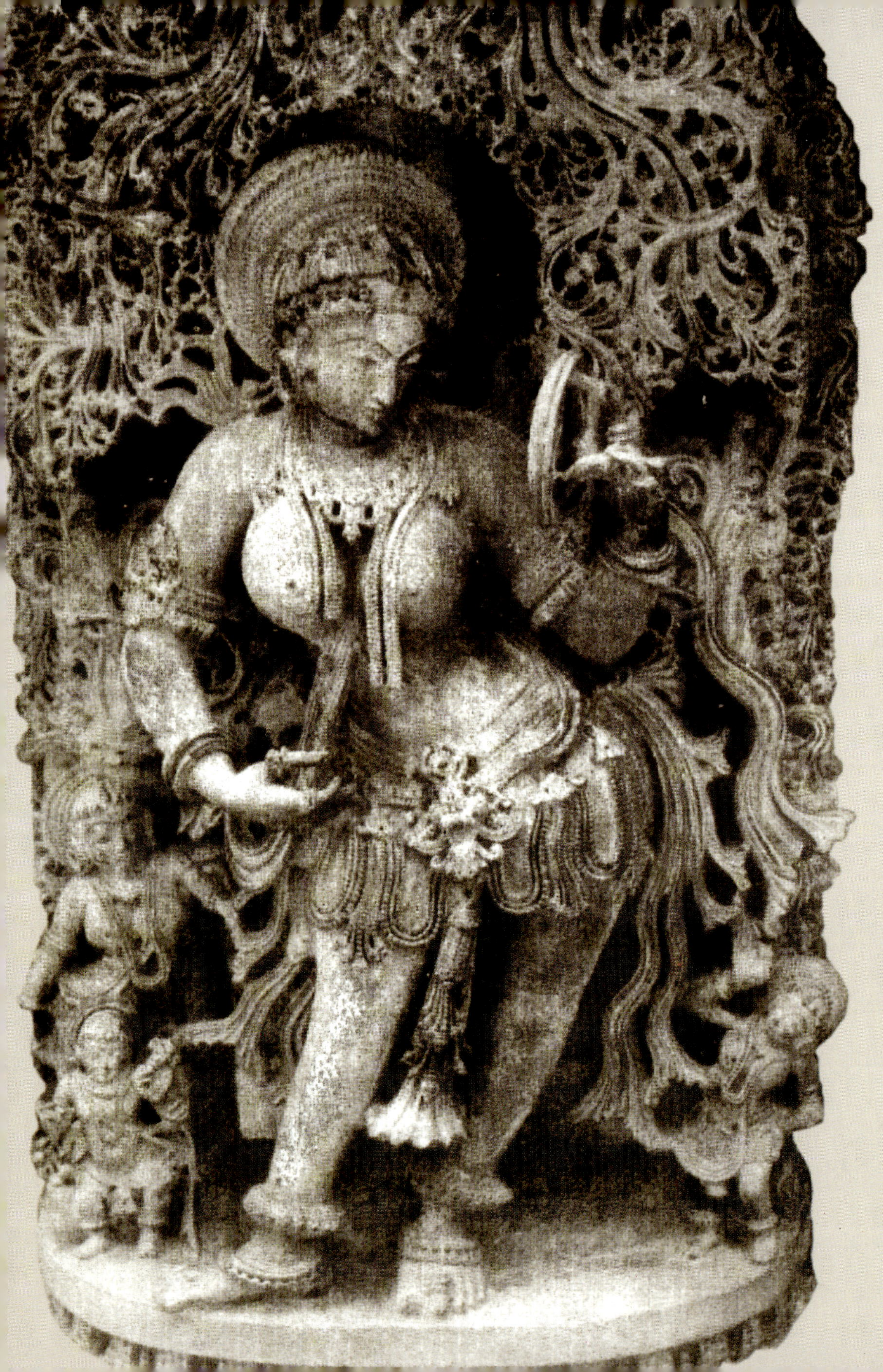

Plate 18. Lady with Mirror Stone, Twelfth Century CE Cennakeśava Temple, Belur

This female figure treated in proper artistic form, imagination and fancy of the sculptor gives its full scope. The damsel contemplating her beauty in a mirror with an attractive pose is a fine example of the delicate touch of the unknown sculptor. This work is a masterpiece of delicacy and of intimate charm, reminding an achievement of art; it has given some of the loveliest commentaries on literary passages and an insight into rich and glorious life of the best of art in India.

This charming young lady in stone calls a near similar description in the *Sāhityadarpaṇa*, IV.12 which runs thus:

अयुन्नतस्तनयुगा तरलयताक्षि द्वारि स्थिता तदपुयानमहोत्सवाय ।
सा पूर्णकुम्भनवनीरज तोरणस्त्रक्सम्भार मङ्गलमयत्नकृतं विधते ॥

ayunnatastayugā taralayatakṣi dvāri
sthitā tadupuyānamahot-savāya ।
sā pūrṇakumbhanavanīraja toraṇasraksambhāra
maṅgalamaya-tnakṛtaṁ vidhate ॥

> That damsel, standing at the gate for celebrating the festival of his return with her pair of very high breasts and tremulous long eyes, achieves, as it were, the auspicious purpose of filled water pitchers, and a garland of blue lotuses.

A fine picture of fancy *pūrṇaghaṭa* and wreath of blue lotuses in the pair of breasts and lovely eyes of the damsel at the gate is referred to in the above lines. And a similar one as mentioned in the *Gāthāsaptaśati* (II.40) runs thus: with her blue lotus-like eyes, running to the road, she sees you come, with her pair of breasts like two auspicious water pitchers placed at the doorways.

Plate 19. Yakṣī, Red Sandstone, Kuṣāṇa period, First-second century CE, Soṅkh (U.P.), Government Museum, Mathurā

इंदीवरेण नयनं मुखमम्बुजेन
कुन्देन दन्तमधरं नवपल्लवेन ।
अंगानि चम्पक दलैः स विधाय वेधाः
कान्ते कथं घटितवानुपलेन चेतः ॥

indīvareṇa nayanaṁ mukhamambujena
kundena dantamadharaṁ navapallavena ।
aṅgāni campaka dalaiḥ sa vidhāya vedhāḥ
kānte kathaṁ ghaṭitavānupalena cetaḥ ॥

— Rudrabhaṭṭa, *Śṛṅgāratilaka*, 2

That creator fashioned your eyes with the blue lotus; your face with white lotus; your teeth with jasmine; your lips with tender shoots; your body with *campaka* blossoms; have made all these in this way, why, O lovely girl, did he create your heart with stone?

The young girl stands in graceful *tribhaṅga-mudrā*. She holds the branch of the tree by her right hand while her left hand is on her waist. The full and heavy pair of her breasts have pearl-strings worn on them and with sportive glances the girl is bent with the burden of her breasts. And her mysterious smile connects her with fertility cult.

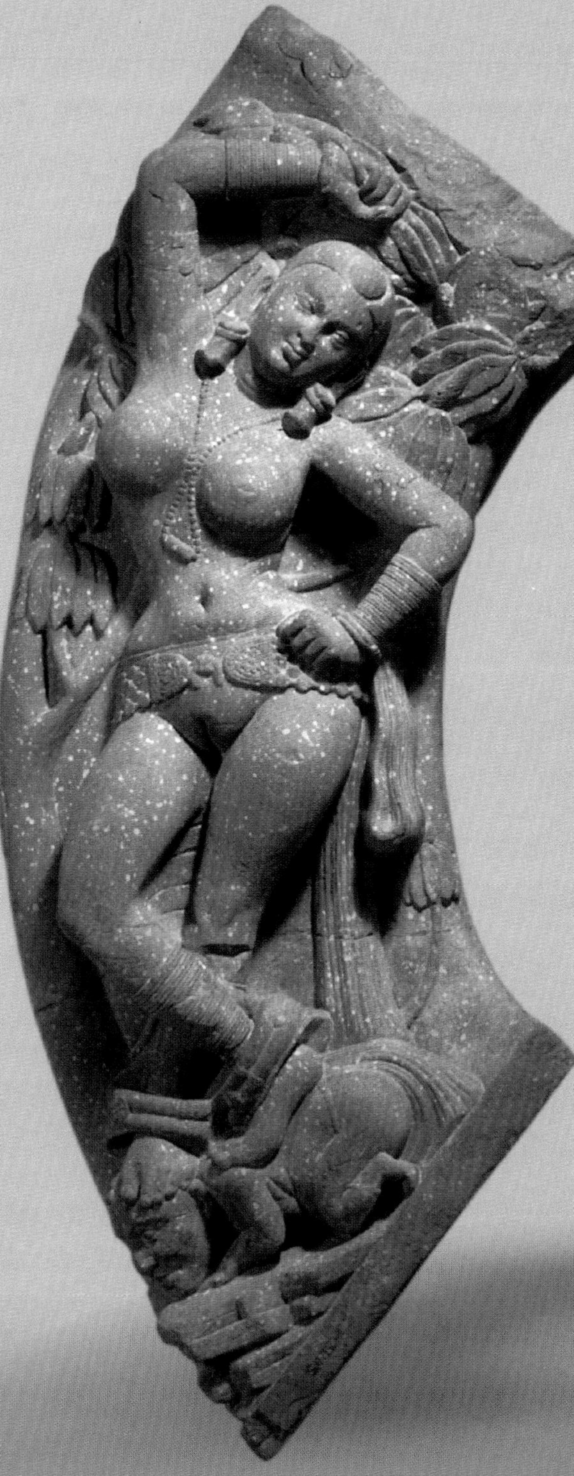

Plates 20 & 21. Standing Yakṣī, Kuṣāṇa period, First-Second century CE, Bhuteshvar (U.P.), Government Museum, Mathurā

कुरंगनेत्रां शरदिन्दुवक्त्रां बिम्बाधरां चंदनगंधलिप्ताम् ।
दृशा गलत्कारुणिकास्त्रयान्तः सम्मोहयन्ती त्रिजगन्मनोज्ञाम् ॥

kuraṅganetrāṁ śaradinduvaktrāṁ
bimbādharāṁ candanagandha- liptām ।
dṛśā galatkāruṇikāstrayāntaḥ
sammohayantī trijaganmanojñām ॥

— Bāṇa, *Kādambarī*, Pūrvārdha, 8

Her eyes are like *kuraṅga* (deer), (here the poet says, she is *mṛgnayanī*) lips red like *bimba* (pomegranate) fruit, and eyes are full of compassion (*karuṇā* — pathos or tenderness); her face lovely like the moon of autumn, the whole body is fragrant with the sweet smell of sandalpaste. She is the one and the only one beauty who touches emotions of worldly people.

Indeed when actually considered the comparison is very apt as the illustration will show.

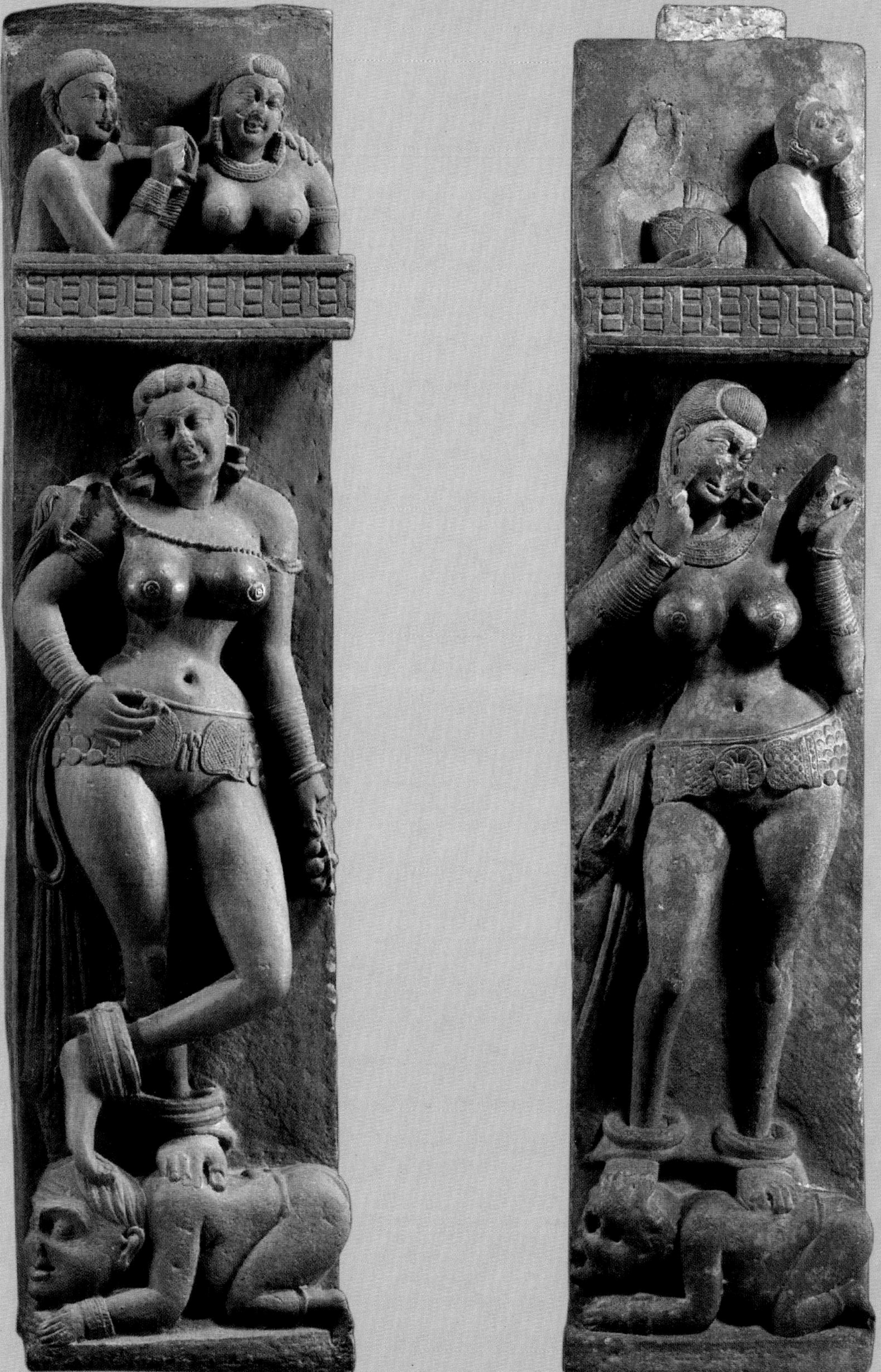

Plates 22 & 23. Standing Yakṣī, Red Sandstone, Kuṣāṇa period, First-second century CE, Bhuteshwar (U.P.), Government Museum, Mathurā

To take the ideal of feminine beauty the verse of Kālidāsa's description of the full breasts without space between them.

अन्योन्मुत्पाड्यदुत्पलाक्ष्याः
    स्तनद्वयं पाण्डु तथा प्रवृद्धम् ।
मध्ये यथा श्याममुखस्य तस्य
    मृणालसूत्रान्तरमप्यलभ्यम् ॥

anyonmutpāḍyadutpalākṣyāḥ
    stanadvayaṁ pāṇḍu tathā pravṛddham ।
madhye yathā śyāmamukhasya tasya
    mṛṇālasūtrāntaramapya- labhyam ॥

—*Kumārasaṁbhavam*, 1, 40

The pair of fair breasts of the lotus-eyed one, with the dark nipples in the centre; so developed rubbing against each other that even a lotus fibre could not go between them, may equally be seen in sculpture where the literary tradition is clearly illustrated visually. The frequent description of the eyes is as resembling the lotus petal and the blue lily.

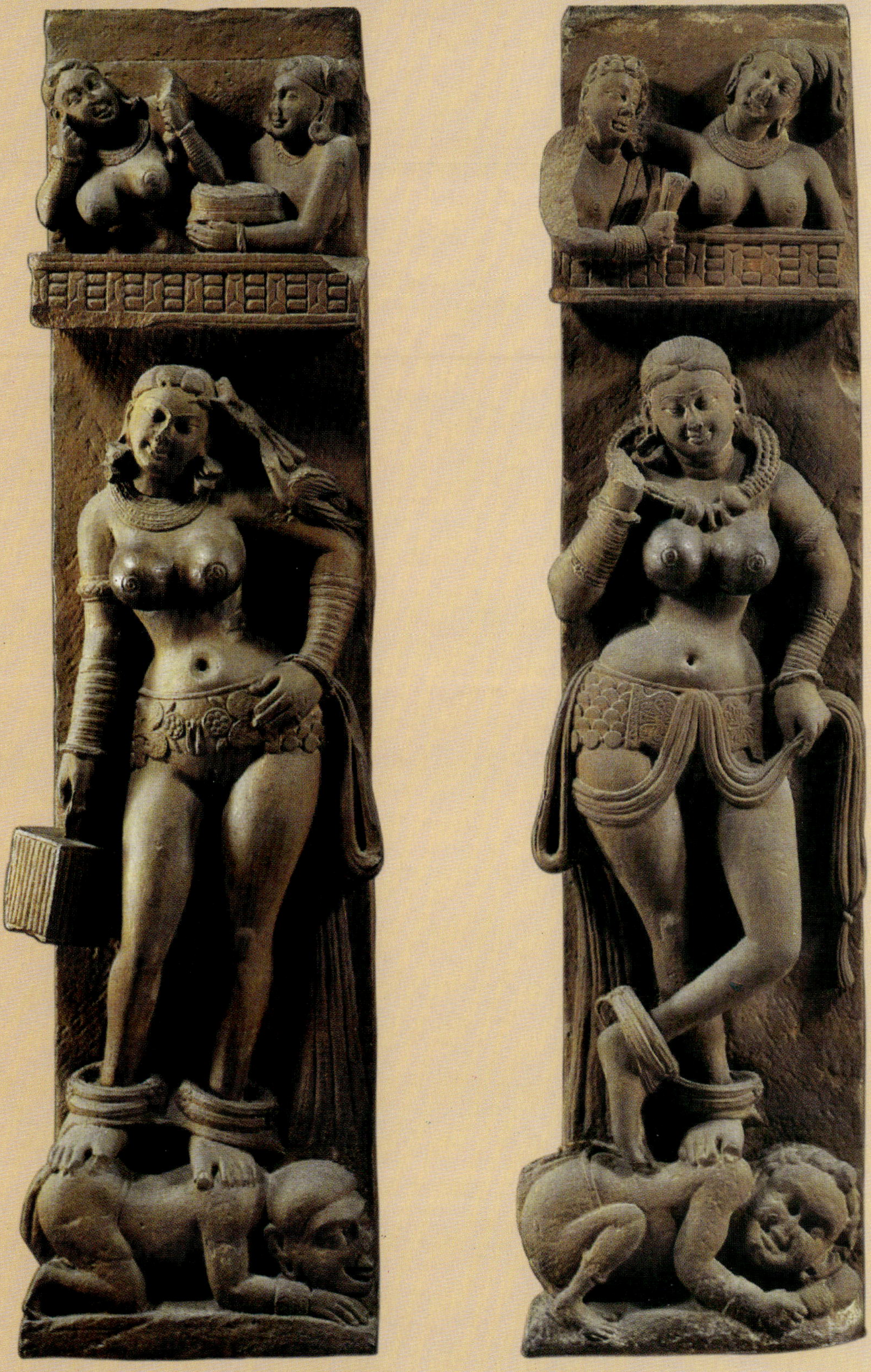

Plate 24: Woman and a bird, Sandstone, Sixth century CE, Rajmahal (Bihar), Patna Museum, Patna

मदनरसमहौघपूर्णनाभीह्रदपरिवाहित रोमराजयस्ताः ।
सरित इव सविभ्रमप्रयातप्रणदित हंसकभूषणा ॥

madanarasamahaughapūrṇanābhīhṛdaparivāhita
romarājayastāḥ ।
sarita iva savibhramaprayātapraṇadita
haṁsakabhūṣaṇā ॥

—Māgha, *Śiśupālabadha*, VII. 23.

Those (Damsels) shown like rivers with their flowing stream of love filling the deep navel lake and flowing past the soft line of hairs above it, with jingling of the anklets surrounding like swans as they moved with graceful sway.

Māgha puts this in very picturesque fashion in a verse describing the turbulent streams of *madana* or love with whirlpools of navel drowning the *romarāji* surrounded with *haṁsaka*s and other jewels, the *haṁsaka*s having a double meaning of anklet and swan as suggestive charm here.

The poem gives this pleasant picture of the flowing stream of *śṛṅgāra, madanarasamahaugha,* as poet puts it, and the damsels are shown swimming in the stream of love.

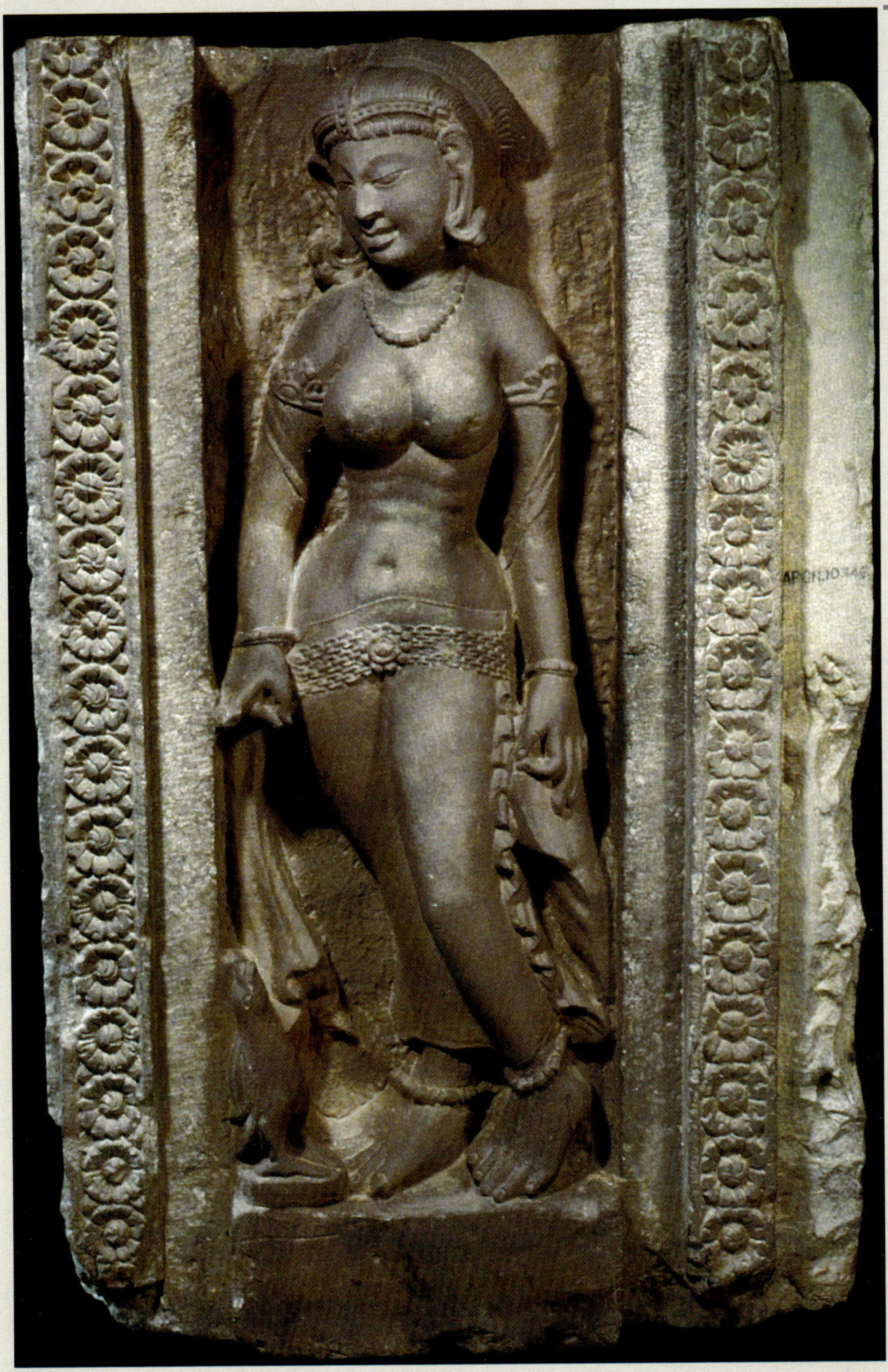

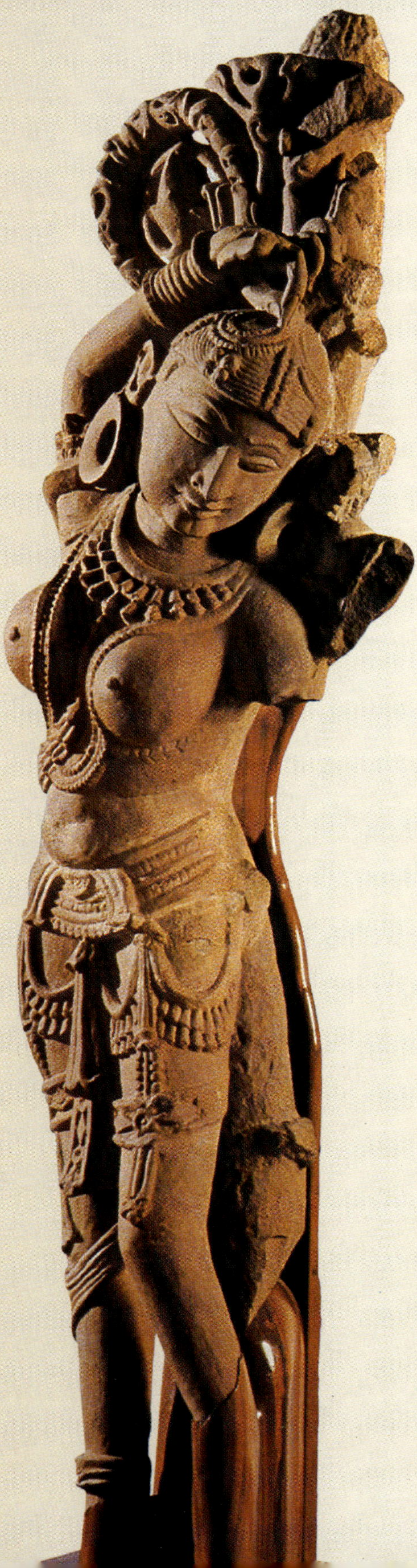

Plate 25. A Celestial Female, Sandstone, Twelfth Century CE

The celestial beauty, standing leisurely is seen engaged in setting up her hair ornament. Sensualism in this modest figure is found exposed only in the treatment of her exposed breast with their charged nipples.

> With their pale checked faces as beautiful as the golden lotus and with their breasts anointed with sandalpaste and having pearl-strings worn on them and with their glances sportive with intoxication, women bent with the burden of their breasts kindle love even in great vowed to celibacy.
>
> — *Ṛtusaṁhāra*, *Sarga* 6, 32

Glossary

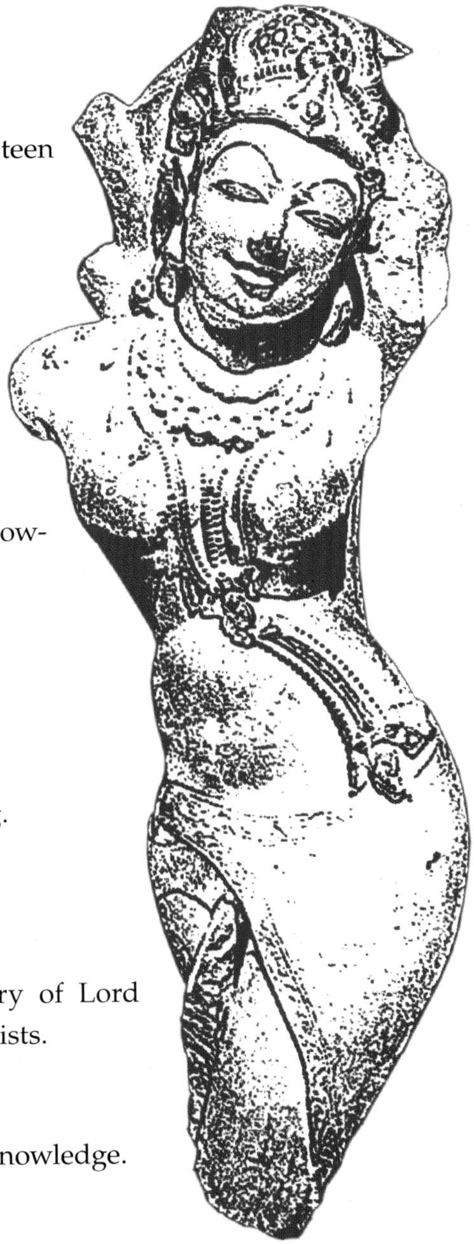

Anūḍhā	:	Unmarried female.
Bālā	:	A girl between ten and fourteen years of age.
Bhagavatī	:	Goddess.
Bhakti	:	Devotion.
Bhāva	:	Disposition, state, mental attitude.
Buddha	:	Perfect enlightenment.
Brahma-Svāda	:	One who has acquired knowledge of divine.
Dakṣiṇa	:	Who love all women.
Dampati	:	Couple.
Devatā	:	God.
Dhṛṣṭa	:	Who does not care for wrong.
Duḥkha	:	Suffering.
Guṇa	:	Quality.
Jātaka	:	Person, previous birth story of Lord Buddha according to Buddhists.
Jāti	:	Caste or variety.
Jñāna	:	Knowledge, philosophical knowledge.

Kalā	:	Art, evolute *varṇa*, it denotes *prakṛti*, *māyā*, absolute transcendental power.
Kāla	:	Time, perceptual units of eternity.
Kāma	:	Desire, passion.
Kanyā	:	Generally, a daughter, virgin between fourteen and sixteen years of age.
Karuṇā	:	Universal compassion.
Kuṇḍala	:	Ear ring.
Mahākāla	:	On the abstract terms of eternity.
Mithuna	:	Lovers in dalliance.
Mokṣa	:	Salvation, liberation.
Nāgaraka	:	Cultural people.
Nāyak	:	Hero.
Nāyaka-Anukūla	:	Sincere and devoted.
Nāyaka-nāyikā bhāva	:	Emotional state between lovers.
Nāyikā	:	Heroine.
Nirvāṇa	:	Salvation.
Ātmā	:	Self.
Padminī, Citriṇī, Śaṅkhinī, Hastinī	:	The Sanskrit literature divided *nāyikā* in four categories according to their *jāti* and *guṇa* experience, nature and physical feature.
Parakiyā	:	Another's.
Paramātmā	:	Supreme Being.
Pratimā	:	Icon.

Prauḍhā : Lady above thirty years to fifty-five years.

Rasa : Sentiment, sap, taste, and juice, *rasa* is also conceived in terms of intense emotional attachment between male and female principles.

Śaiva : Relating to the God Śiva, a member of Śaiva sect.

Śakti : Energy.

Sādhanā : Term for spiritual exercise.

Sahaja : Natural, it is also the term for ultimate reality.

Sāmānya : Common.

Saṁsāra : World.

Śaṭha : Unkind and false.

Śrī : A goddess of abundance, fertility, blissful prosperity, luck and beauty.

Śriṅgāra : Decoration.

Sufī : Believer of the cult of mysticism among Muslims.

Svakiyā : One's Own.

Tāla : Beating time in music.

Taruṇī : A young girl from sixteen to thirty years.

Uḍhā : Married woman.

Upāsanā : Worship.

Vaiṣṇava : Relating to Viṣṇu, worshipping Viṣṇu.

Vṛkṣakā : Dryad.

Vyākhyāna : Speech, Lecture.

Yakṣī : Celestial nymph.

Yoga : Disciplining of the body for various purposes, physical, mental and spiritual.

Yogī : Follower of the *yoga*.

Yogic : Related to the *yoga*.

Bibliography

Anand, Mulk Raj and Lance Dane, *Kāma-Kalā*, New York, 1958.

———, *Kāma-Sūtra of Vātsyāyana*, New Delhi, 1982.

Apte, Vamana Shivarama, *Sanskrit-Hindi Kośa*, Varanasi, 1966.

Aśvaghoṣa, *Buddhacarita*, tr. E.H. Johnston, rpt., Delhi, 1972.

Basham, A.L., *A Cultural History of India*, London, 1975.

Bhanudatta, *Rasamañjarī* (Hindi), Bombay, 1926.

Bhattacharya, N.N., *The History of Indian Erotic Literature*, New Delhi, 1975.

Chaturvedi, Sita Ram, *Kālidāsa Granthāvalī* (Sanskrit-Hindi), Varanasi, 1980.

Coomaraswamy, Ananda K., *Art and Craft of India and Ceylon*, London, 1913.

———, *Cultural Heritage of India*, vol. I-V, Kolkata.

———, *The Origin of the Buddha Image*, New Delhi, 1972.

Datta, R.C., *Prācīn Bhārat Kī Sabhyatā Kā Itihāsa* (Hindi), Allahabad, 1966.

De, Sushil Kumar, *Ancient Indian Erotics and Erotic Literature*, Kolkata, 1959.

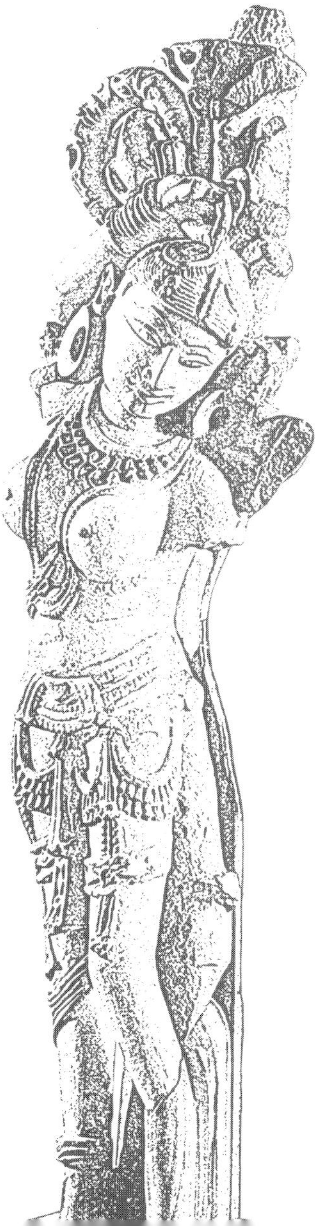

Desai, Devangana, *Erotic Sculpture of India: A Socio-Cultural Study*, New Delhi, 1975.

Deussen, Paul, *The Philosophy of the Upaniṣad*, rpt., New Delhi, 1979.

Fouchit, Max Pol, *The Erotic Sculpture of India*.

Gāthā Saptaśatī, by Satavahan Hall, Mumbai, 1933.

George, Christopher, *The Candamaharaṣaṇa Tantra*, New Haven, 1974.

Gichner, Lawrence, *Erotic Aspects in Hindu Sculpture*, USA, 1949.

Gordon, D.H., *Pre-Historic Background of Indian Culture*, Bombay, 1958.

Ghosh, *Aesthetic Theory and Art*, Delhi, 1979.

Gupta, Shyamala, *The Beautiful in Indian Art*, New Delhi, 1979.

———, *Art, Beauty and Creativity*, New Delhi, 1999.

Havell, E.B., *Ancient and Medieval Architecture of India*, 1915.

———, *Ideals of Indian Art*, London, 1911.

History and Culture of Indian People, ed. R.C. Majumdar, A.D. Pusalkar and A.K. Majumdar, vol. 1-10, Mumbai.

Huntington, L. Susan, *The Art of Ancient India*, New York, 1985.

Kāmasūtra, tr. Indra Sinha, London, 1980.

Keith, A.B., *R̥gveda Brāhmaṇas and Aitareya and Kauṣītaki Brāhmaṇas of the R̥gveda*, 1920.

Keith, A.B., *Taittirīya Saṁhitā*, Varanasi, 1967.

———, *The Karma Mīmāṁsā*, London, 1921.

———, *The Religion and Philosophy of Veda and Upaniṣad*, Varanasi, 1965.

Kosambi, D.D., *Myth and Reality*, Mumbai, 1962.

———, *The Culture and Civilization of Ancient India*, New Delhi, 1962.

Lesson, Francis, *Kāma Śilpa*, Mumbai, 1962.

Marshall, J., *Mohen-jo-daro and Indus Civilization*, London, 1930.

Pal, Pratapaditya, *The Sensuous Immortal*, London.

Pant, Ramesha Chandra, *Early Hindu Civilization*, Kolkata, 1963.

Pusalkar, A.D., *Studies in the Epics and Purāṇas*, Mumbai, 1955.

Raghavan, V., *R̥tu in Sanskrit Literature*, New Delhi, 1972.

Randhawa, M.S., *The Cult of Trees and Tree-Worship in Buddhist-Hindu Sculpture*, New Delhi, 1964.

Ray, Niharranjan, *Idea and Image in Indian Art*, New Delhi, 1973.

R̥gveda (in Hindi), ed. Satavalekar, Paradi, 1983.

Saundaryalaharī, ed. A. Kuppuswami, New Delhi, 1991.

Sharma, R.S., *Aspects of Political Ideas and Institutions in Ancient India*, New Delhi, 1959.

Sharma, R.S., *Indian Feudalism, 300-1200*, Kolkata, 1965.

Sivaramamurti, C., *Sanskrit Literature and Art — Mirror of Indian Culture*, New Delhi, 1955, *The Art of India*, New York.

Standard English-Hindi Dictionary, 2nd edn., Allahabad, 1983.

Shukla, Ramachandra, *Hindi Sāhitya Kā Itihāsa* (Hindi), Kāśī, VS 1919.

The Age of Imperial Kanauj, eds. R.C. Majumdar, A.D. Pusalkar and A.K. Majumdar, vol. 4, Mumbai.

The Amaruśataka of Amarūka, ed., Durga Prasad, Mumbai, 1916.

Thomas, P., *Kāma Kalpa on the Hindu Ritual of Love*, Mumbai, 1959.

Tripathi, L.K., Erotic Scenes of Khajuraho, Bulletin of the College of Indology, Banaras Hindu University, No. 3, 1959-60, Varanasi.

William, M., *A Sanskrit-English Dictionary*, London, 1956.

Zimmer, H., *Myths and Symbols in Indian Art and Civilization*, U.S.A., 1963.

———, *The Art of India Asia*, New York, 1955.

Index